THE CRACK HOUSE RESCUE

Disclaimer

The information and advice contained in this book are based upon the research and the personal experiences of the author. They are not intended as a substitute for consulting with a healthcare professional. The publisher and author are not responsible for any adverse effects or consequences resulting from the use of any of the suggestions, preparations, or procedures discussed in this book. All matters pertaining to your physical and mental health should be supervised by a healthcare professional.

THE CRACK HOUSE RESCUE

Raising a Granddaughter and Saving a Daughter from Addiction

Julia Savell

THE CRACK HOUSE RESCUE, Savell, Julia

First Edition

Subtitle: *Raising a Granddaughter and Saving a Daughter from Addiction*

❖❖❖ THREE SKILLET
www.ThreeSkilletPublishing.com

Scriptures marked AMP are taken from the AMPLIFIED BIBLE AMP): Scripture taken from the AMPLIFIED® BIBLE, Copyright © 1954, 1958, 1962, 1964, 1965, 1987 by the Lockman Foundation Used by Permission. (www.Lockman.org)

Scriptures marked GNB/GNT are taken from the GOOD NEWS BIBLE (GNB): Scriptures taken from the Good News Bible © 1994 published by the Bible Societies/HarperCollins Publishers Ltd UK, Good News Bible© American Bible Society 1966, 1971, 1976, 1992. Used with permission.

Scriptures marked KJV are taken from the KING JAMES VERSION (KJV): KING JAMES VERSION, public domain.

Scriptures marked NIV are taken from the NEW INTERNATIONAL VERSION (NIV): Scripture taken from THE HOLY BIBLE, NEW INTERNATIONAL VERSION ®. Copyright© 1973, 1978, 1984, 2011 by Biblica, Inc.™. Used by permission of Zondervan.

Scriptures marked NKJV are taken from the NEW KING JAMES VERSION (NKJV): Scripture taken from the NEW KING JAMES VERSION®. Copyright© 1982 by Thomas Nelson, Inc. Used by permission. All rights reserved.

ISBN: 979-8-218-03168-8

Table of Contents

Dedication

I dedicate this book to Kelli Christine Williamson. This book may be painful to read in the beginning, but your testimony glorifies our Lord and Savior due to the miraculous healing that took place in you. I also dedicate this book to Melodi Williamson. Your inner beauty and maturity amaze me. Thank you to my husband, Aaron Savell. Your love and support mean everything to me.

To the addict: You are not meant to live a life of torture and suffering. Let God's love lift you and set you free. To those who love an addict: You are not alone. Keep the faith and fight the good fight.

Introduction

This book is 100% true. I may have left out a name or two or gotten some of the dates off a bit, but everything written actually happened. The God of the Bible still speaks to the hearts of His followers. He still heals His people. There is a real enemy in the world who seeks to steal, kill, and destroy. Drug use and addiction are powerful tools the enemy uses to destroy lives and families. The Lord can and will deliver us from evil if we trust in Him completely. Read His Word and call out to Him. Open your heart and allow Jesus Christ to change your life.

Ephesians 6:12 (KJV): *For we wrestle not against flesh and blood, but against principalities, against powers, against the rulers of the darkness of this world, against spiritual wickedness in high places.*

Hebrews 11:6 (NKJV): *But without faith it is impossible to please Him, for he who comes to God must believe that He is, and that He is a rewarder of those who diligently seek Him.*

The Crack House

I PULLED up to my daughter's low budget apartment complex in southeast Texas on a warm winter afternoon in January. My daughter Kelli lived in a small, two-room apartment with her boyfriend and her baby, Melodi. I had arranged to pick up my thirteen-month-old granddaughter and take her home with me to visit for a few hours. I love being around children so much, especially babies. I felt so excited for the chance to spend time with my very first grandchild, Melodi Rain.

I visited Kelli's apartment at this current location once before with great disappointment. She moved around often. She did not keep relationships long, so every few months she moved to be with another friend or new boyfriend when she either wore out her welcome or got into a bad argument. She made friends easily, but due to an abundance of drama in her life, she had difficulty keeping them. The prior visit to Kelli at this apartment left me unsettled and questioning her ability to raise a newborn baby. I yearned for a better life for her. *Could there be drug use, some type of abuse, or child neglect going on?* In the back of my mind, I suspected things were not right. I had every reason to be suspicious of illicit activities occurring from prior experience with my daughter. I could never be sure about what went on in Kelli's life, as she remained allusive and secretive. My daughter and I did not have a close relationship. I wanted one, but we led very different lives. Now she had a little baby girl to raise, and I hoped and prayed she had turned her life around and become more stable. She promised me many times that she had made some changes.

Kelli and the baby lived there with Kelli's new boyfriend, Daniel. He had not fathered baby Melodi, but for the time being had stepped in as a father figure. Compared to Kelli's past choices of companions, I felt this young man had potential. From what I could tell of him so far, he seemed a bit of a step up from her usual boyfriends. When my husband and I met Daniel, he told us that his parents were Spirit-filled Christians, who raised him as a Christ follower, attending church often. Faith in God meant so much to my husband Aaron and me. Daniel seemed like a nice young man but had no job. How could he help provide for Kelli and her baby with no income? Kelli frequently ended up with unemployed boyfriends. The young man did look attractive and clean cut, even though he was very thin, and he dressed nice, unlike any of her past boyfriends. Each of Kelli's previous boyfriends had a fairly similar look. For the most part, they were usually rough-looking, white males, scrawny and short in stature, frequently sporting a buzz haircut, and wearing dirty, raggedy clothes. Most of them appeared to be what we call in Texas poor, white trash. For the life of me, I could not fathom why such a beautiful and smart young lady like my daughter would choose to be in relationships with the likes of these men. Deep down, I appreciated that looks did not matter to Kelli, but I wanted her to have the confidence to surround herself with upstanding people.

As I continued toward Kelli's apartment, I climbed the two flights of outdoor stairwells and approached the door. I knocked and waited a few seconds. No answer. I was used to that when visiting my daughter. I usually had to wait quite a while for her or one of her roommates to answer the door. Sometimes they did not answer at all. I had an uneasy feeling this time, as I stood at the front door. Unfortunately, it would only get worse. I knocked several times and prayed for someone to answer. Kelli expected me. She had agreed to let me come pick up little Melodi for an afternoon visit. I really wanted to see my granddaughter. My intuition told me that things were not right, and I could not wait to have my little grandbaby and get her out of that environment, even for just a few hours. I knocked again, louder this time. No answer. I waited a few more minutes and knocked again, very loudly, practically banging on the door. Finally, I heard some stirring around inside. I knocked again. *Please answer*, I thought. Still, no one came to the door. "I know someone is in there," I huffed to myself. I knocked one last time, very loudly, and called out, "It's Kelli's mom, Julia. I'm just here to pick up baby Melodi." Finally, someone came to the door.

Standing there on the porch of Kelli's apartment, on that warm sunny day, the door finally opened, sweeping a feeling of darkness and depression toward me. I did not know the young person who came to the door, so I smiled and introduced myself as Kelli's mother. I told her that Kelli said I could come over and pick up my granddaughter for a while. She looked at me suspiciously, so I assured her that I just wanted to get the baby quickly and I would be on my way after that. The young lady, looking hesitant about letting me in, opened the door slowly and only part way and moved aside to let me in.

The inside of the apartment looked dreadful and shocking to me! I did not know much about crack houses, and I sure did not think my daughter would live in one. I did my best to appear nonjudgmental as I glanced at the horrible appearance inside. *Is this a crack house?* I wondered. I sensed that the person who let me in felt uncomfortable with my presence. I walked into the small, dark living room, barely finding a place to take a step, as the floor was absolutely covered from wall to wall with various piles of stuff, mostly piles of clothes. Some of the clothes piles stacked up as high as my waist. There were also many big black trash bags all around the room. Some seemed to be stuffed with clothing, and others filled with garbage. A large sliding glass door that led out to a little patio on one side of the room had a thick curtain drawn, blocking out almost all the sunlight. The darkness from the room matched the dark feeling enveloping me as I walked further into the apartment.

Right in the middle of the cramped living room, a woman slept on a hide-a-bed, pulled out from the couch. That explained the curtains being drawn in the middle of the afternoon, but I still had an unexplainable "dark" feeling upon entering the dwelling. The sleeping woman stirred a bit as I entered. The person who let me in turned on a dim lamp in the living room. My concern grew as more light shone in the room. The woman on the hide-a-bed sat up a little bit after the light came on. Although she looked to be only thirty-five or forty years old, she had long, straggly, gray hair, like an old granny. She looked a bit odd. Something did not seem right about her, besides just being half awake. As a curious person, I wondered why she would still be asleep, in the living room of my daughter's apartment, in the middle of the afternoon. I did not quite understand why my twenty-year-old daughter would have this older lady hanging out with her and sleeping in her living room at this time of the day.

The person who let me in never introduced herself but informed me to be careful where I walked because they had a new puppy in the apartment that was not house broken yet. She apologized and said there might be some dog poop on the floor. I looked down to the left of where I stood and saw a fresh pile of doggy doo-doo laying there. I felt quite sickened! I scanned the room, and did my best to sound nonchalant, "Oh, that's okay. I know how it is," I said, with a little laugh. I tried to hide my utter shock and disgust, as the person seemed very leery of my presence there. I felt relieved, though, that she finally let me in, after so many minutes of knocking and waiting on the front porch.

The apartment also included a very small dining room area with a table and a half wall that led into a small, narrow kitchen. I noticed two or three other mounds of dog business on the floor. My heart grew weary as I looked around. Trash and clutter covered almost every square inch of the apartment, including the tables and counters. *How could anyone live like this?* Mounds and piles everywhere!

All around the dark, smelly living room, dining room and kitchen I saw piles of trash, mounds of dirty dishes and cups, piles of papers, wadded up bags, dirty ash trays filled to the brim, dog poop, and other items all around the room from top to bottom. I felt sick to my stomach! My little grandbaby had recently learned how to crawl and toddle around. Growing babies need to be on the floor, exploring their environment. My goodness, the idea of letting her crawl around in this filth, in this dark, dirty, depressing place made me want to cry! I could not stand the thought of that, but despite my horror, I continued to try to act normal. I asked if my daughter Kelli was there and explained again that I was only there to grab little baby Melodi up and take her for a visit.

The young lady led me down a short hallway, past a bathroom on the left and a closed door on the right, to an open door of a bedroom at the end of the hall. I looked in the room and saw traces of natural light coming in through a window, but, like the rest of the apartment, this bedroom also had piles of clutter, clothes, and trash laying around in it. Inside the room, I noticed a little nightstand with a small lamp and a bed that was actually just two mattresses stacked up on the floor. I saw my daughter Kelli and her boyfriend Daniel asleep on the bed. The person who let me in announced my presence to Kelli. She got up out of the bed and greeted me. She told me she would get Melodi up and ready to go soon, but that she needed to get dressed first. She directed me to go on into the other bedroom door to see Melodi, who was asleep in her crib. "She's taking a nap?" I asked. Kelli told me that Melodi was not taking a nap but was still sleeping from putting her to bed the previous night. I felt a little surprised and confused by that and said, "Wow! She's still asleep? It's past one o'clock in the afternoon."

"She's been asleep since about seven-thirty pm last night," Kelli said. I gave my daughter a very puzzled look and said, "What?" *That did not seem right.* Kelli gave an apologetic shrug and answered, "She always does that. I put her to bed at about seven-thirty most nights, and she's still asleep at this time the next day." I furrowed my eyebrows in a confused look at Kelli. Under normal circumstances, I knew that babies who fell asleep at seven-thirty pm at night, would most likely wake up at about six or seven o'clock the next morning. I realized that babies required extra sleep, about twelve hours a night, but not eighteen hours. That did not make sense. This new revelation added to my fear of little Melodi not getting proper care. Kelli excused herself to go to the restroom and I let myself into baby Melodi's bedroom.

As I slowly opened the door, sadness filled my heart as I looked around the room. *Well, at least this is consistent to the rest of the apartment*, I thought. Piles of junk and clutter covered the entire floor of the nursery, wall to wall, and I struggled to even find a place to step into the room. I saw piles of toys, high stacks of clothes, and bags of trash. An enormous cushion lay in the middle of the room, amongst all the other clutter, and covered more than half the floor space in the medium-sized nursery. The room smelled of urine, and I noticed dirty diapers laying around on the floor as well. I seriously wondered how I could get over to the crib on the opposite side of the room from where I stood in the doorway with all the stuff covering the floor. I felt lost and bothered. The immense, difficult trek to get over to my baby granddaughter through all the clutter and trash felt symbolic of my feelings in my gut. I sensed a growing physical and emotional separation from my daughter and granddaughter. I started to walk over piles of toys and attempted to get around the huge cushion on the floor without stepping on it. I took the longest stride possible but could not avoid catching my foot on the cushion and almost fell. It seemed like an obstacle course! I just wanted to get to my little granddaughter and rescue her from this terrible situation. My heart hurt for her so badly. After almost pulling a muscle from taking such huge strides to walk across the floor without tripping, I finally reached the crib. I made it to my little baby Melodi, laying on her stomach, still asleep.

I fought back the tears as I looked at her, because I could tell that she been in that crib for far longer than necessary. It did not take a genius to figure out the neglectful scenario. Baby Melodi's blanket did not cover her, but lay wadded up beside her, next to the edge of the crib. Two empty baby bottles and a couple of stuffed animals lay in the crib by her as well. She only had on a t-shirt and diaper. A wave of despair rushed into me as I looked at the diaper completely filled and on the verge of bursting open. My daughter Kelli talked previously of Melodi suffering with a bad diaper rash. Of course she did! No wonder!

I reached down into the crib and gently touched her back. The baby stirred and gave out a little low-pitched cry. I could assume that she had probably cried out several times throughout the morning, but nobody came to get her, recalling earlier that I had knocked and knocked, and then practically banged on the door for quite a while before I was let in. My heart felt broken as I pictured my precious little granddaughter crying in her crib, needing her basic needs met, with no response. Crying for love, crying to be fed, crying in pain from a diaper rash. *How long did she cry out? For minutes? For hours?* My eyes welled up with tears at these thoughts as little Melodi finally woke up and got up on her hands and knees and pulled herself up to a standing position on the rails of her crib. She looked at me and gave me a big smile. What an extremely beautiful little baby! I gazed at her petite little frame, her fair skin, her blonde, baby-fine fuzzy hair with her sweet big, blue eyes.

I got little Melodi out of the crib and wanted to put a clean diaper on her, first thing. Seeing no changing table, I laid her on the floor. Her bottom looked worse than I thought it would. She had patches of thick, brownish, reddish color skin from her diaper rash. I tried to clean her little bottom off with the diaper wipe, but she gasped and cried in pain. I shook my head and knew that the alcohol in the wipe stung baby Melodi's skin, so I took some wipes and rinsed them in warm water at the kitchen sink and tried again. Kelli came in the room as I finished diapering the baby and said, "Yeah, Melodi has a bad diaper rash. I don't know why it's so bad, poor little thing." I swallowed the lump in my throat and held in the tears I felt coming due to my anger toward Kelli and my sympathy for sweet little Melodi. I ignored Kelli's comment. I knew exactly why she had that rash. They neglected the poor baby, leaving her abandoned in the crib for hours after waking up every morning, laying in a dirty diaper all that time. Anger welled up in me, but I held my tongue. I just wanted to get Melodi cleaned up and dressed, so I could rescue her out of that horrible dark, depressing place of neglect. I did not want to get into a discussion with Kelli at that time. She thought she had me fooled with her innocent act and probably thought I was clueless to any problems with baby Melodi. As far as she knew, I believed everything was going well with her and the baby. Everything was far from fine, and I knew a bad situation when I saw one. Sweet little Melodi was not being taken care of properly. I needed a chance to think things through before speaking to Kelli about my concerns. Most of all, at that moment I really wanted to get my granddaughter out of that apartment, and take her to a nice, bright, clean place, where I could shower her with love and spoil her, like she deserved.

I packed a few diapers and some clothes for Melodi in my purse, and Kelli walked me downstairs to the parking garage to her car, so we could get the baby's car seat. I held little Melodi close to my chest and she hugged my neck so tight. At just thirteen months old, this sweet, precious baby craved love and attention so desperately.

We got the car seat in my car and buckled up Melodi. I asked Kelli if it was okay if the baby stayed overnight at my house, if she did not cry too much, and Kelli said it would be fine. As we drove away, I adjusted the rearview mirror so that I could watch baby Melodi as I drove, or see the back of her little head, at least. I felt relief and happiness as we drove away from that dreary place. I also felt sadness knowing her visit would last only a day and that I had to bring her back to that dreadful apartment soon.

Melodi and I arrived at my house shortly. We lived a

quick ten-minute drive down the road from Kelli and her boyfriend. Oh, what a thrill to have my sweet grand-daughter there with me in my home. My husband, her step-Papa Aaron, my son, her Uncle Randy, and our new little Border Collie mix rescue puppy Panda greeted baby Melodi and me when we arrived. After saying, "Hi!" to everyone I immediately got little Melodi in the bathtub to bathe her. Her clothes smelled musty, and her face looked dirty, with patches of white, dried milk around her mouth and on her cheeks. I placed her in the warm bath water. She winced and cried when I washed her diaper rash area with soap and water, poor baby, but I knew it would feel better afterward. I put some clean clothes on her that I had bought to keep at my house. The last time she came to my house, she did not have any clean clothes. The clothes Kelli packed for her usually had a musty smell and reeked of old cigarette smoke. She looked adorable and so comfortable, dressed in her colorful matching shirt and pants that I got her. I loved seeing her pink cheeks, and silky, baby-fine, blondish-white hair.

Then we took time to play and enjoy our time together. I felt so happy to have my sweet, precious grandbaby girl there with us, and planned to pamper her and spoil her and shower her with love and attention. I would read books to her, play on the floor with her, sing to her, rock her in the rocking chair, hold her and snuggle with her. I wanted to feed her healthy, yummy snacks and meals and give her some warm formula and juice. I would keep her clean and hoped to nurse her diaper rash back to healthy, clear skin. The stark reality saddened me though. I was only going to have her for a day, at most. My heart broke every time I pictured her in that shabby crib in that messy room, where she had been left for hours by herself, probably crying herself back to sleep, losing hope that someone would come rescue her, feed her, and care for her. My heart felt weary picturing the stacks of clutter and trash and dog poop on the floors of her little room and the rest of the apartment, with no space to crawl around or attempt to stand up and take her first steps. My heart ached thinking about the floors of Kelli's apartment, and how literally every square inch of floor space was covered, leaving no room for a curious, healthy baby to explore, learn, and grow happily.

I brought little Melodi into our living room and placed her on the carpet with the little collection of toys I had gotten her. I sat down on the floor with her, and we had so much fun as we played with the little musical baby toys, little plastic and rubber figures and dolls, and, of course, our dog Panda, just a puppy at the time. Melodi laughed and crawled around. She chased after Panda and tried to grab her with her tiny little baby hands. When Melodi was not chasing Panda, the puppy ran after the baby. As a young pup in the teething and biting stage, she playfully nipped at the baby several times. Most of the time it tickled Melodi, but a few times little Panda got a good enough nip of her ankle or leg to bring Melodi to tears. I stayed close, constantly monitoring them, and separating them from time to time. They were so cute and I probably took about a hundred or so pictures. My husband teased me when we looked back at the pictures I took of Melodi and Panda that day. Aaron said the pictures looked like stop-motion photography because I took so many. He joked that if the pictures were pieced together, they could make a little film. We laughed at that!

That evening I read several nighttime story books to baby Melodi as I held her in my lap in a rocking chair. Then I rocked her in my arms for an hour or so until she fell asleep. I never wanted to let her go. I knew she would be back in the dark, depressing, dirty apartment tomorrow. My heart felt heavy. She should not be in a place like that. She needed more attention. She should not be left crying in a crib for hours. My daughter said that Melodi slept-in until the late afternoon every day. She acted like that was normal behavior for a baby. I did not believe that, especially after seeing the bad diaper rash on the baby's skin. I had the feeling she was lying in a soiled diaper, crying with no response for much too long, probably every day. I felt pretty sure that Kelli neglected to care for Melodi properly.

Due to Kelli's past, I suspected that she and the others at the apartment most likely used drugs, stayed up most of the night, and slept for half of the next day. That explained the woman asleep on a hide-a-bed in the living room in the middle of the afternoon, with all of the curtains closed. I wanted so badly to believe my daughter when she told me she had "cleaned up her act". Years later, Kelli confirmed that the apartment was indeed a "crack house", and that the prematurely old-looking lady sleeping on the hide-a-bed in the living room was their drug dealer.

My daughter, who was nineteen at the time, had been using drugs since her early teens, and even ran away from home at the young age of eleven years old. She struggled a great deal mentally for most of her childhood and teenage years. She had been a hyperactive child with ADHD, attention deficit disorder with hyperactivity, and struggled with self-esteem issues and feelings of rejection. At only eleven years old, she smoked marijuana for the first time. She started doing other drugs as well and began to get into trouble at school and at home. As a teenager, she went back and forth from living with me and her stepdad, to living with her father. She started hanging out with the wrong crowd. She became very rebellious and did not want to follow any rules set by her stepfather and me, or her father, and ended up moving in with her boyfriend at the age of seventeen. We did not approve of that at all and tried to get her to come back home. Kelli tried to convince us that she and her boyfriend would stay in school and that they were living successfully together. Her boyfriend Keith was a high school classmate, and the two of them did continue going to school together, at first. A short time later though, she told us that he had been abusive toward her. She would not go into much detail about it, and still refused to come back home. What happened a couple of weeks later was bone chilling and horrifying.

One night, back when Kelli was in high school and lived with her boyfriend Keith, at about 2:00 am in the morning, I awoke to a phone call. I answered it and heard my daughter Kelli whispering. I could barely hear what she was saying. "Hello? Kelli? What's wrong? What's happening?" I asked.

"Mama, can you come and pick me up right now, please?" Kelli whispered, in a desperate voice. "I can't talk right now," Kelli said in a hoarse whisper, "I snuck out of the apartment and I am so afraid Keith is going to come and find me. He's been hurting me, Mom, and I'm so scared right now. Can you just please come right now and get me,

Mama? I'll be outside in between my apartment and the one right next to it."

"Yes," I replied, alarmed, and fully awake by this time, "of course. I'll be right there."

"Please hurry, Mama!" Kelli said quietly, sounding fearful and panicked.

I will never forget the look of sheer terror on my baby girl's face when I pulled up into the parking lot of their apartment complex in the dark of night a few minutes after receiving Kelli's panicked phone call for help. Running for her life, I saw the look of sheer terror on her face as she came sprinting toward my car from about a hundred yards away. It turned out that her boyfriend Keith was a psychotic, manipulative young man with trust issues. When he suspected that Kelli cheated on him, he recruited several of his friends to join with him in performing a gang abuse plot against my daughter. Among other acts, they finished their abusive tirade by completely shaving her head bald to "teach her a lesson". Such sick, twisted brutality! I was saddened and disturbed to find out what had happened to her. My daughter ran up to my car with a shaved head, barefoot and wearing only a tank top and shorts in the middle of a cold night. She did not dare go back into the apartment to retrieve her things for fear that the psycho boyfriend would trap her and keep her there against her will.

"Go, Mama! Go, go, go! Quickly! Please drive away before he sees us!" Kelli said, looking around in utter fear, humiliated and broken.

All I wanted to do at that point was grab my little girl and hug her, but I could tell that she was in danger. The look of fear and desperation on her face as she came running toward my car was so shocking and scary and became burned into my memory. She was literally running for her life. For several months after that, I had to push the dreadful thoughts of "what ifs" out of my mind, thinking about what would have happened to her if I had not answered the phone that night. When we got to my house, I just hugged her and held her while she cried in my arms. My husband and I never approved of that boy Keith from the start, but I knew that moment was not the time to say, "I told you so," to Kelli. I just thanked God that she was safe now and hoped that she could heal from this.

2

The Rescue

KEITH was Kelli's boyfriend from the past. Shortly after she escaped from Keith's abuse, Kelli found that she was pregnant. Kelli and Keith did not get back together, thankfully. Kelli had her first child, Melodi, and then a few months later, she started living with Daniel in the trashed-out apartment. I had picked up my granddaughter from Kelli and Daniel's apartment to spend some time with her and felt very leery about their living conditions. I suspected Melodi did not receive the proper care she needed from her mother.

Melodi spent the night at my house and did a great job. She fussed a bit more than I remembered her doing in the past, but she seemed pretty happy for the most part. I loved having her there. She was such a joy. That night we sat in our rocking recliner and I rocked her to sleep. She seemed to enjoy having me hold her, and I loved having her in my arms. I decided my "grandmother" name would be Mimi Juju. As we rocked, I prayed, "Dear Lord Jesus, I love You and I know You love us, my sweet little granddaughter and me. Father, I feel so unnerved after seeing Kelli's apartment today. Please help Melodi, Father. You see the condition of the apartment that she is living in, Lord, and it just breaks my heart to think of her having to go back to that place. Please make a way for her to live in a nice, clean environment. I pray that she can get all the attention and love she needs to thrive and be healthy and happy in a peaceful atmosphere. Please make a way for this, Lord, even though there seems to be no way right now. I pray in Jesus' name, amen." Tears streamed down my face as I poured my heart out to the Lord, something I did on a regular basis. The baby slept peacefully in my arms, and I never wanted to let her go.

The next day we attended a family gathering, a birthday party for my dad, at my parent's house close by. My extended family and I frequently got together to celebrate birthdays and holidays, as we all lived in close proximity to each other, and shared close relationships. I took my sweet little Melodi over to my parents' house. My daughter Kelli joined the party as well. Kelli and I enjoyed the company of our family, as we ate, talked, and joked around. Baby Melodi crawled around on the living room floor in the middle of the family gathering, and we enjoyed watching her play, while we visited with one another. Melodi was actually the first of many great-grandchildren to come for my mother and father.

Our family gatherings usually went on for several hours. During the course of the day, Kelli and I ended up on the back porch, in the back yard of my parents' house. They had a pool in their large back yard and my sisters and I, along with our respective families, enjoyed spending a lot of time there, having pool parties and watching our kids play outside. On that day in late January, we did not swim, but still enjoyed sitting outside in the mild afternoon of the Texas Gulf Coast. Kelli and I sat down on wicker chairs by a glass table with an umbrella, while I held baby Melodi. Kelli asked if she could talk to me privately and I told her, "Sure, of course."

Kelli confided in me that she and her boyfriend Daniel struggled lately with many verbal arguments. She explained that this happened almost daily, and often escalated into episodes of shouting and screaming at each other. She worried about the effect on Melodi and her well-being from this volatile environment. Kelli also told me she planned to possibly break up with her boyfriend Daniel.

My mind immediately went back to my prayer from the prior night. I prayed for God to make a way for my little Melodi to live in a nice place with a nurturing and loving environment. *This may be the perfect opportunity for me to get my grandbaby out of that place*, I thought to myself.

In the spur of the moment, I decided to have a heart-to-heart talk with Kelli. I realized I had to think quickly and make sure I worded things very carefully. I knew my daughter well enough to know she could be very defensive and stubborn at times. If I questioned her ability to raise Melodi properly, she would most likely become offended and angered. I worried that this would cause her to retreat from me and seek advice elsewhere. I feared my window of opportunity to help little Melodi would close very quickly if I did not word things subtly and unobjectionably. The next idea I had, I believe, came from the Lord in an answer to my prayer from the previous night.

Through a divine whisper, I thought about suggesting that Melodi come stay with me for a little while. I figured it would be even better if Kelli felt that *she* came up with the idea of having Melodi come live with Mimi Juju for the time being. I did not want her to become offended and think I was attacking her mothering skills, so I had to be careful how I worded things.

I expressed my deep sympathy and regret that she and Daniel struggled with this problem of arguing. I told her that I noticed that little Melodi did seem a bit more sensitive and fussier than she had in the past, possibly from being around people yelling. Then I silently said a little prayer to the Lord for guidance, and continued, "Kelli, do you think it might be better for you if Melodi comes and stays with me for a few weeks while you and Daniel figure out what you want to do? Maybe that will make it easier for you to deal with things and make a plan for yourself."

Kelli quickly answered, "Well, yes, I do think that might be a good idea. That might help me to figure this whole thing out. That might be good, Mama." I nodded at her and hugged baby Melodi tight in my arms, amazed at how she agreed to that arrangement so quickly.

"Wait!" Kelli snapped, her face suddenly showing some irritation, "You're not just trying to take Melodi away from me, are you?" she said, looking very suspicious.

Oh no, I said to myself, *I knew that was way too easy.* I feared Kelli's defense mode might cause her to backtrack. *Will she make it harder for herself and possibly hurt the baby's chance of living a better life, just because she thinks that I am judging her?* I wondered. She had quickly agreed to letting Melodi stay with me temporarily, but now I worried she would change her mind and not let Melodi come stay with me after all. I did not want the poor baby to stay in that unhealthy environment. I knew I had to word things very carefully. I wanted her to think that it was *her* idea and not mine. Her lifestyle choices and addictive personality often caused her to become defensive and suspicious about things. She acted out irrationally and impulsively made poor decisions for herself when she thought someone did not approve of her or judged her actions.

"No, Kelli," I tried to assure her, "this would only be for a couple of weeks. I'll only keep her for a short time, so you can break up with Daniel, or whatever you decide to do, and you won't have to worry about Melodi living in a volatile environment while you go through these changes," I explained. "You can use a little time to work things out for yourself." I gave her a smile and put my hand on hers. "And it's only if you want to, of course. Just for a little while, or as long as you need."

Kelli looked down, her shoulders seemed to relax, and then she looked back up at me and smiled. "Yeah, Mama," she whispered, "I think that would probably be a good idea."

I felt so relieved that Kelli agreed to let me take Melodi for a while. Within the next week or so I moved Melodi into to my house. Kelli said that Melodi would only need to stay with me for a few weeks to a month or so, at the most. Deep down in my heart, I suspected that the new living situation would most likely last longer than a month, and could possibly even become a permanent arrangement if things did not change drastically for Kelli. She had not maintained a healthy lifestyle and I doubted that she could suitably raise another human being and give the proper mental and physical care needed. She may have convinced herself that she had a decent life, and she could raise a child with success. I did not know if she believed that or not. I was not sure how she felt about it. The drugs definitely clouded her judgement. Kelli probably needed to convince herself that she only needed me to take care of Melodi for a few weeks, to keep from feeling like an inadequate mother because she could not take care of her own baby. We did not discuss her feelings that much. Her willingness to let Melodi stay with me without much coaxing gave me a pleasant surprise, and I hoped my daughter knew, deep down, that she made the right decision and was doing what was best for her baby. Either way, I felt such relief and joy that Melodi would come stay with me now in a safe, happy place, and not in that depressing, filthy "crack house" anymore.

Graciously, my husband agreed to let Melodi come stay with us. My husband and I spoke previously about the improper care Melodi received and the unacceptable living conditions my daughter provided for her. He sympathized with the anguish I felt when I had to take our sweet baby granddaughter back to Kelli's apartment after having her for a few hours, and he knew it broke my heart thinking about the neglect. I thanked God that my husband Aaron had such a charitable, soft heart and allowed me to take her in, not knowing how long she would be there with us. I told him what I told Kelli, that it may just be for a month or so, but I felt like he knew that it would most likely be longer, maybe even indefinitely, as I did.

Aaron and I had become the sole caretakers of our fourteen-month-old granddaughter, on the cusp of becoming a very busy toddler. We knew this new arrangement would change our lives momentously. I feared it could become very overwhelming if we thought about it in excessive detail. I did not want to worry myself or my husband, so I attempted to downplay the possibility of it being a permanent situation in my discussions with my husband. Even with myself, I tried to only think ahead by a few days or a couple of weeks at a time.

My husband and I both worked full time, and I needed to find childcare for Melodi immediately. I took a few days off work to do this. Thankfully, our finances enabled us to afford to enroll her into full-time childcare, despite the enormous increase that childcare centers charged for tuition since my children were little. I raised my three children as a single mother for several years before Aaron and I married. None of my children attended a daycare center, except for about a year when I worked as a preschool teacher. Other than that, I babysat children in my home professionally, so that I could keep my children home with me full time, while still earning a living. Therefore, the significant rise of monthly expenses, mostly from the cost of putting Melodi in a daycare, really surprised Aaron and me.

After several days of researching and visiting schools, I found a nice daycare for our new full-time addition. I set her up for her first day of daycare and planned to go back to work on a Monday morning. I will never forget Melodi's first day in the little school. It felt like one of the longest and most agonizing days of my life! I brought Melodi to the Harbour Side Daycare and signed her in at the front desk. I carried her down the hall and found the door to her classroom. I looked into the little window in the door and the young lady inside motioned for us to come in. The young lady, the toddler-age teacher, remained seated on the floor and gave us a friendly greeting. I introduced my granddaughter to her new teacher and let her know that Melodi had never attended this or any other daycare before. Melodi looked very scared and insecure as I placed her gently down on the floor in the little classroom, close to her new teacher and some other toddlers. She looked up at me with trepidation and lifted her arms, motioning for me to pick her up. Her eyes got real big and started to tear up. She did not actually start crying, but she looked so frightened. As I started to walk away to leave, she did not take her eyes off me and she seemed so confused and dejected. I smiled at her, blew her a kiss, and told her that I loved her and would be back in a few hours to pick her up. I knew from my childcare teaching experiences that the longer the "goodbye" dragged out, the harder it became for the child to adjust to their parent leaving, so I made a quick exit from the room. I briefly peered through the little glass window of the classroom door and saw Melodi's sorrowful eyes and a bewildered look on her face, and my heart felt crushed as I turned to leave. I contemplated the fear and confusion Melodi experienced in that moment. I fully understood the difficult emotional adjustment she presently faced by leaving her mama and the only home she knew up to that point just a few days prior. Regardless of the poor conditions of her previous environment, leaving a familiar place, at any age, always proved a challenge, and now, she found herself, literally, just plopped down in a strange new place, with people she did not know.

I got into my car and headed to work with the feeling of a weight on my shoulders and the vision of Melodi's confused, sad face burned into my memory. At work in a public school as a fourth-grade teacher, I had a very busy day as usual, but I could not shake the grieving thought of leaving little Melodi at the daycare that morning, knowing that she had no idea why I left her there. Many mothers had felt this way countless times. I knew that. *Come on. If I could just make it through this day*, I thought, as the hours seemed to drag slowly on. *Ugh! I can't wait to get my little Melodi!* I said to myself. I pictured myself dashing out of my car when I got there, grabbing her up, and holding her forever. *Only 7 hours left*, I counted down. *Only 3 hours left*, I noticed. *Only 1 hour left*. Finally, the workday ended, and I could leave! I felt so relieved. Poor baby! I imagined it had to have been a long day for her, too.

I drove as quickly as I could, without exceeding the speed limit enough to risk getting a ticket. That would just slow things down; otherwise, I would have gone faster, if I could have gotten away with it. The whole way to the daycare, I envisioned Melodi's sweet face in my head. I remembered her look of rejection and confusion as I left her sitting on the floor that morning. I felt her fear and sadness. I drove for about thirty minutes and finally arrived at the little daycare center. I quickly went in, signed her out, and walked straight back to her class. I opened the door, greeted the teacher, picked up Melodi, listened to the brief account of her day, thanked her, and walked straight to my car in the parking lot. At last, I finally did what I had been craving to do all day, since the moment I had left that sweet little girl in her new classroom. I put her diaper bag down, swiveled her around, from my hip to my front, and just embraced her for about five minutes. My sweet little Melodi melted into my chest, threw her arms around my neck, and sobbed. Unable to verbally express her feelings at that age, I knew she had experienced the same anguish as I had that entire day but was now so overjoyed and relieved to be in my arms. I never wanted to let her go! I will never forget how powerful that hug felt as we began an amazing grandmother and granddaughter connection that day.

Melodi grew accustomed to going to the daycare. After a week or two, she began to understand that I always came back to get her later, and her fear faded when I dropped her off on the days I worked. When we were together, I gave that sweet little girl so much attention! I attempted to make up for affection and care that she possibly missed during the first few months of her life. My generous husband suggested we change one of the rooms in our home into the baby's nursery. It had been his office and studio. He had been using the room to work on his music, store musical equipment and bass guitars, and he had his desk, personal computer, files, and other things to help run the household set up in that room. He unselfishly moved all those items and furniture into our bedroom. I am thankful for my loving, patient husband, who sacrificed so much for me and our granddaughter.

After we settled the logistics of taking the child into our home, and creating a safe, happy environment for her, I worked on providing a healthy mental atmosphere as well.

As a graduate of early childhood development, I knew that daily routines and schedules contributed to children's happiness and security. Our nighttime routine became a favorite ritual Melodi and I shared together. Each night after dinner, I bathed her and dressed her in comfortable jammies. I bought a used rocking chair, the classic wooden model, and we sat in it together each evening. I loved the peacefulness of cuddling with her in that rocking chair every night. As we rocked, I read to her from a variety of toddler books and children's classic storybooks, mostly borrowed from our local library. This tradition of sharing story time came from my wonderful mother who read to me often as a child. I still vividly remember many of the stories and books my mom read to me sitting in her lap in the living room rocking chair as a youngster. I also picked out many books to read to Melodi that I read to my own children throughout their childhood. I absolutely loved reading children's storybooks and nursery rhymes to her and cherished our time we spent in the rocking chair every night. Books are so magical! I read my granddaughter five to eight short books per night. Some of our favorites included *The Frog and Toad Are Friends* series, Doctor Seuss books, *The Berenstain Bears*, *The Snowy Day*, *Goodnight Moon*, The *Madeline* series, *Little Bear*, Richard Scary's *Busytown* books, Little Golden books, and various *Mother Goose's Nursery Rhymes*.

To continue our nighttime ritual, after reading several storybooks, I turned down the lighting, and I sang to her as we continued rocking. I sang whatever came to mind, ranging from nursery rhymes, folksongs I learned growing up in the 1970s, or songs from Sesame Street and other children's programs that I loved in my youth. I sang anything from old-time church hymns to classic Americana songs, to lullabies. My life and passion always revolved around music and singing. My three sisters and I grew up with music and sang together for our parents and neighbors from the time we were old enough to talk. My wonderful mother and father exposed us to a wide variety of music and had it playing in our household at all times. My siblings and I grew up listening to so many styles of music, such as jazz, classical, folk, rhythm and blues, soul, rock and roll, and country and western, as well as contemporary popular music. Some of my mother's favorite artists included Harry Belafonte, Neil Diamond, Tom Jones, the Andrew Sisters, Judy Garland, and Nat King Cole. Nobody topped my mother's absolute favorite artist, the one and only Elvis Presley, in her eyes. She talked about the legendary "king of rock and roll" as though she knew him. In fact, every time an Elvis Presley song came on the radio or if he appeared on the television, my mother good-humoredly had her children proclaim, "Elvis is the king!" My father exposed us to good old country and western music such as Johnny Cash, Patsy Cline, Dolly Parton, Merle Haggard, Willie Nelson, and Conway Twitty. I picked several songs and lullabies to sing to Melodi every night, each one bringing beautiful memories to my recollection. I sang for twenty minutes or more as we rocked and I held her in my arms. I wanted nothing more than for her to feel love, comfort, peace, and happiness.

To end my nightly ritual with Melodi, I laid her down in her little bed and said a prayer for her. As I prayed, I rubbed her back or brushed her hair back with my hand.

Lastly, I turned on the compact disc player to instrumental lullaby music and set it to repeat all night at a low volume. I kissed her on her cheek and closed the door as she drifted into slumber. I continued this entire ritual for her bedtime every single night, finding it very relaxing and pleasant myself. I enjoyed it just as much as she did, I believe. Melodi always stayed in her bed all night and slept soundly and peacefully in her own bedroom.

Despite the joy I experienced from taking over full-time care of my granddaughter, and the satisfaction that came from seeing so much growth in her, I started feeling exhaustion set in. I came to realize it was a much greater challenge raising a toddler in my forties than it was when I was twenty years younger, raising my own three children. I continued my full-time job as a schoolteacher as well, a very hands-on, exhausting profession in itself. However, I had no regrets about taking in and raising my granddaughter. I was determined to push through the difficulties and fatigue and do the best I could.

Unfortunately, even though I completely took over caring for my daughter's child, I once again started falling into a mental trap that had begun in my mind a few years prior. I allowed the enemy of God, thus my enemy, the devil, to badger me in my thoughts and imaginations. The devil tricked me into feeling condemnation for what had become of Kelli's life. I blamed myself for the path Kelli chose of using drugs and eventually spiraling downward to meth and heroin addiction. I called myself a terrible mother. I not only listened to the words and lies of my soul's enemy, but I believed them, and repeated them often to myself, several times a week and sometimes on a daily basis. *I am a terrible mother,* I told myself. *All of Kelli's problems arose because I gave birth to her when I was too young. I raised her wrong and had horrible mothering skills,* I thought.

I cried all the time about the current troubles that Kelli endured and blamed myself. Kelli had so many challenges and problems she faced in her life. She could not settle down and grow roots. She constantly had to move and change jobs frequently. Her social life was a mess. People came in and out of her life due to her lifestyle. She lost friends often, got taken advantage of by them, and even ended up being abused or beaten up sometimes. So-called friends stole things from her, or sometimes, she robbed from them, and at times, she falsely received blame for pilfering items. I never knew what to believe. She received many DUIs and DWIs, tickets for driving under the influence and driving while intoxicated and landed in and out of jail several times. Kelli rarely took accountability for any of these problematic issues, bad choices, and cases of drama with friends and coworkers. She claimed innocence in all of the job losses and struggles with the law. Little by little, despite my knowing better, I got into a rut of secretly faulting myself for Kelli's poor life status, believing the accusation in my mind, that it was all due to my failure in raising her properly.

The devil, in my mind, continued to blame me relentlessly. I cried more and more. I prayed to God often and asked Him to help Kelli and heal her and deliver her, but I incessantly repeated to myself mentally, the phrase, *I am a terrible mother!* Tears streamed down my face, as I lay in my bed or hid in the bathroom, attempting to hide my sadness from the rest of my family and husband. I constantly repeated the mental torture with cruel declarations to myself, again and again, *I am a rotten mother! I ruined Kelli's chances of happiness and success in life because I did a horrendous job of raising her.* At the time, I did not feel contrite about saying this to myself. I accepted these statements as the cold, hard truth and felt I deserved to suffer mentally for the troubling lifestyle I brought upon my daughter. Kelli fell into an addicted lifestyle at the age of fifteen. While she suffered for years, I suffered as well, blaming myself and torturing myself mentally with hateful self-talk.

The devil is a liar! He tried to destroy me by stealing my joy and the most precious thing to me, my children and my belief in myself as an excellent mother. The Bible describes him in 1 Peter 5:8 (KJV) saying, "Be sober, be vigilant; because your adversary the devil, as a roaring lion, walketh about, seeking whom he may devour." That credent brought me down for a long time, but thankfully God stepped in. Ultimately, about seven years into Kelli's drug addiction spiral, I received a beautiful message from the Lord one day while I prayed and cried out to Him, and the words changed my life forever. He mentally spoke peace to me, in my mind and heart, and explained that all the "self-talk" I had been doing, all the words of blame, shame, regret and self-hate were not my own words at all. I had not been talking to myself. The hateful speech I perceived in my mind came from the enemy of my soul, the devil himself. The devil had been disguising himself and speaking to me in my mind, making me think it was my own inner voice. The devil was the one verbally abusing me, trying to bring depression on me, and ultimately attempting to destroy me. I should have known! The Bible says that the devil comes to steal, kill, and to destroy. "I have come [says the Lord] that you might have life—life in all its fullness" (John 10:10, GNT). The Lord reminded me that I am His child, the daughter of a King, and dearly beloved! He enlightened me with this news and encouraged me to recognize the devil as the enemy of my soul, and to stop listening to his evil lies!

This clear, life-changing message delivered to me from the Lord opened my eyes to the schemes of the devil and gave me an amazing revelation! My heart and soul began a wonderful healing process that day. Kelli's condition did not improve at all at that point, however, *my* life changed drastically. I began the process of triumphing over my soul's enemy and attaining inner peace such that I had not experienced in years. I started living a life of joy again. From that day on, when I heard what I previously thought to be my own inner voice accusing me of being a rotten mother and that all of Kelli's problems stemmed from my poor parenting skills, I proclaimed, "Shut up, devil! You are a liar! I am not going to listen to you anymore." In fact, I counteracted the lies and accusations with a completely different type of inner speech. I literally started speaking to myself words of encouragement. Instead of rude, hateful lies, I talked to myself about my outstanding mothering characteristics, and mentally listed all of the wonderful things I did with my daughter Kelli and her younger sister, Tiffani, and their little brother, Randy Junior.

I finally understood the stress and mental burdens I held onto by blaming myself for Kelli's waywardness needed to stop. I knew all along that I did not fail as a mother, but in fact showed great love and attention to Kelli and my other two children since their birth. I started making it a habit to counteract the devil's lies by reminding myself several times a week about all the great mothering qualities I had and the love I gave my children all their lives. Not only did I love them, hold them, nurture them, and care for their physical health, but my children and I also had many special routines and traditions that we shared. I taught them important life lessons daily, through discussions and by example. I shared life with my children throughout their childhood and talked to them all the time. As a "hands-on" mom, I loved my children unconditionally. I knew the power of touch and I held my babies constantly. I absolutely adored each of my children! Especially as a baby or toddler, I loved holding and snuggling with each of them and rocking them in a rocking chair at times during the day and every night as part of our bedtime routine.

I also reminded myself about the fact that I raised my children in church. I myself had strayed away from church and had forsaken my relationship with God as a teenager, but from the very beginning of my pregnancy with Kelli, as an unwed young adult, I answered the call of the Lord to come back to Him. Finding out that I was pregnant, and knowing that I would have to raise a child as a single parent is what motivated me to recommit my life to God. I joyfully started attending church regularly, two to three times a week, and felt my spirit come alive once again. I became very active with several groups and programs our local church offered, and became close friends with several fellow church members, as well as my sister Margie, who had become a born-again Christian. My wonderful sister is who encouraged me to give my heart back to the Lord. As a single mother, I always brought my little ones to church and put them in the Sunday school classes and children's church. When they got a little older, I had the girls join Missionettes and I put Randy in Royal Rangers. These were Christian girl and boy scout programs. As teenagers, my children actively participated in the youth ministries through my encouragement. My three children enjoyed acting and singing in the church Christmas programs and attended the camps offered by the church every summer. I talked to them often about God, read the Bible to them, and explained Biblical stories in interesting, age-appropriate ways. We prayed together as a family and I prayed with each of them individually often. I assisted each of my three precious children in receiving salvation by teaching them to pray what we Christians call "the sinner's prayer", asking Jesus Christ to be their personal Savior. I waited until each one seemed spiritually ready to understand the meaning of salvation before explaining it to them. I did not force any of my children to pray the sinner's prayer, but only offered to them its meaning. Each of my children individually asked if I could help them pray and receive Jesus as their Savior at different ages of their lives.

I knew the benefits of staying close to my extended family and raising my children around them, as well. We never lived far from my mother and father, Grandpa Gordy and Grandma Frankie. My three sisters and their families lived within a few miles of us as well, so my children knew all of their cousins and had close relationships with them and their aunts and uncles. We got together for almost every major holiday and celebrated all of our birthdays together. We had impromptu swimming parties and backyard barbeques at my parents' home, the house I grew up in, several times throughout the summer. My two girls and son rarely went to any "babysitters" other than my parents or sisters. Our whole family stayed very close, and my children flourished from having loving ties to their grandparents, cousins, aunts, and uncles.

Besides family, God, and motherly nurturing, another special gift I gave to my children involved reading to them every day. I loved reading books to them! Books, books, books! I bought books for them from the Scholastic Book Club when I could. I frequently took them to our local public library and checked out dozens of books every few weeks. We loved visiting the library weekly in the summer when they were out of school! They played in the children's section of the library with blocks, puppets, and toy cars, or sat at little tables and drew pictures. Then I read several picture books or chapter books while they sat on my lap in the little wooden rocking chair at the library near our home. We checked out a stack of books to take home and read at bedtime or after breakfast. I loved sharing books with my children so much, and I even taught Kelli to read at age four and taught Tiffani when she was three years old. I had worked at a Montessori school for a couple of years and learned how to teach reading to toddlers by observing the teacher there who used the Montessori method. My girls enjoyed learning to read and caught on quickly. My son, however, did not enjoy the process as much. He did not appreciate sitting still for long, and often became distracted by his toy cars or stuffed animals. I gave it my best shot, but my son had more fun jumping off of the edge of the couch or running around in the yard. He loved sitting in my lap and letting me read books to him but learning to read came later with his kindergarten teacher.

My life improved dramatically after hearing a Word from the Lord to stop listening to lies of condemnation I had once thought to be my own inner voice. I continued practicing self-encouragement by listing noble details, stories, and characteristics of my past child-rearing days until it became a habit. The deceitful devil could not disguise himself to me anymore and call me a "horrible mother" using my own voice. I thanked God for com-municating this revelation to me, through His still, small voice. I appreciated the precious times I spent with all of my children and the wonderful memories we shared, especially when they were young. My children meant more to me than anything else, and still do, other than my relationship with the Lord and my husband.

I realized, of course, that I was far from being a perfect mother and that I had indeed made many mistakes, but I decided not to dwell on the mistakes of my past and to forgive myself, as I knew the Lord had. I had conceived and birthed Kelli out of wedlock and never married her father. I met and married my first husband three years later. Although we met in church, I did not give myself enough time to really get to know this man before agreeing to marry him. Unfortunately, we had a poor marriage, almost from the start, that only lasted seven years. He fathered my second and third child, Tiffani and Randy, Jr. After failed attempts at reconciliation and counseling, we split up due to his infidelity. I raised my three children by myself for a few years, but the Lord always took care of us. Then I met and married the love of my life, my second husband, Aaron. This man stepped up as a tremendous stepfather to my three children, right from the start, and fulfilled my dream of having a wonderful, Godly husband.

Thereafter, when the enemy attempted to accuse me of being a horrible mother, again and again, I stopped listening to the hateful words. I recognized the devil as a liar, and the father of lies, who disguised himself and tricked me, for a season, into thinking I heard my own internal voice spewing false accusations and insults about myself. I took control of my thoughts and inner voice, and obeyed what my loving Father, the King of kings, impressed upon my heart to do instead. I made a point to reminisce about all the wonderful things I did with my three sweet children and the marvelous times we spent together on a daily basis, year after year. I focused on the love I poured into them as children and throughout their teenage years, and the lessons of life I taught them, through word, example, and experience. My emotional and spiritual healing did not happen instantaneously, but eventually, over a period of several months, the accusing thoughts ceased in my brain. The Lord healed me mentally and spiritually through a methodical process of reversing the accusations of failure. I became healed because I heard the voice of God and chose to obey Him. He renewed my mind through His love and grace, by reading His Word and through my communion with Him on a daily basis. This gradual, permanent healing brought me inner peace and allowed further growth in my spiritual well-being and happiness.

Among other things, I applied the words of the Bible

from Romans 8:1 (KJV) to my life, "There is therefore now no condemnation to them which are in Christ Jesus, who walk not after the flesh, but after the Spirit." Even though Kelli remained an actively practicing drug addict, I gave glory to God for healing my mind, and thanked Him that I did not have to wait on a change in circumstances to attain mental wholeness.

3

Raising a Granddaughter

WHEN Melodi turned three, I enrolled her in the childcare program at the elementary school where I taught fourth grade. The school's childcare program cost several hundred dollars less than the daycare she previously attended, a nice bonus. This pre-school program for employees of the school district and for children with special needs in the community enabled children not yet old enough to start kindergarten to attend school. Melodi loved it and did so well in her class. She loved her teachers and the structure of the program. Her favorite activity was getting to play in the "House Center", a big area in her classroom with a little play kitchen and furniture like a little house. It included play food, dress up clothes, little baby dolls and baby beds, and many other items for the children to use to make believe they were keeping house. Melodi loved so many aspects about her new school and constantly shared with my husband and me stories about her little friends and getting to play in the "House Center". I sincerely loved having her attend the same school as me.

Melodi and all of her classmates greatly benefitted from the inclusion aspect of her new pre-school class. Her class included some physically and mentally challenged children and Melodi loved each one of them dearly. She became especially close to four-year-old Owen, a little boy with Down syndrome. Melodi played with Owen every day. Her teachers informed me that she loved to help Owen with daily routines, and Melodi told me that she taught him to talk. She expressed that he did not speak very well when she first joined the class, but that her little friend started repeating words she spoke to him, enabling him to learn many words and phrases. I believe this wonderful class-room experience of inclusivity during her pre-school years taught her a great deal about life and helped instill compassion and understanding of all people with a variety of challenges and needs.

At the age of five or six years old, however, Melodi started to perceive a difference between herself and her peers that began to bother her. She could not help but notice that most of her friends lived with their mother and father, while she lived with her grandmother and grandfather instead. She started letting this difference disturb her and feelings of animosity crept in. Unfortunately, she blamed the one closest to her, her Mimi Juju, as she called me. This difficult phase really challenged her emotionally and made it hard for me as well. I could not believe it. I worked so hard to rescue her, nurture her, and raise her in a loving, safe environment, and yet, she began to have feelings of resentment toward me. I certainly empathized with her feelings, but it just did not seem fair. It really bothered me.

Deep down, in some ways, raising Melodi kind of felt

like a second chance to raise my daughter Kelli. I provided my granddaughter with so much. My financial situation had greatly improved since the time of Kelli's childhood. I bought Melodi nicer clothes, we travelled more, and we enjoyed outings like the boardwalk, the museum, and the zoo more often because we could afford more. I bought her more books and nicer toys. I had a deep passion for my granddaughter to feel love, happiness, and mental stability, despite having a drug addicted, erratic mother, as well as an absent father until she turned four years old. I loved Melodi so much and treated her as my very own daughter. She reminded me of her mother in many ways, such as her physical appearance, her voice, and her mannerisms. I practically regarded Melodi as my own daughter and gave her as much love and attention as I did my own children when they were young.

When Melodi started acting resentful towards me because her mother could not raise her, it hurt deeply. This new challenge was not something I expected. I relied on prayer and patience and sought Godly advice often. Melodi's mother made matters worse by showing up sporadically, often stirring up chaos within the family. After appearing every now and then, she would disappear, and not be heard from again for another three weeks to several months later. Kelli also called on the phone out of the blue sometimes, to talk to Melodi or ask her to come spend the night with her at any number of various locations. Each of these incidents caused disruption in the growth occurring in Melodi's well-being. She "talked a good talk" to Melodi, but never followed through with her promises. She built up hopes of a permanent reunion with Melodi, but never followed through with the plans. I am pretty sure that Kelli also put ideas in Melodi's head that I purposefully kept them apart from each other, just to be selfish. When Kelli and I spoke, she often alluded to the idea that I took Melodi away from her without good cause. Despite these accusations, she never made any serious attempt to get her daughter back. She never lived in one place for more than three or four months at a time, switching from living with different boyfriends or staying with random friends. When not unemployed, she worked at low paying jobs and only stayed at them for a few weeks to a month or two at a time, then got fired or left jobs without good reason. She often engaged in arguments with coworkers, or just quit, claiming they had an unbearable work environment. She almost never took responsibility or accountability for losing a job or for having to relocate so frequently.

The inconsistent and sporadic pattern of visitation continued with Kelli. She rarely answered our phone calls when Melodi or I tried to contact her. Kelli just showed up from time to time and requested to take Melodi for a night or two. I hesitated to allow it, remembering their living conditions during baby Melodi's first year. Unfortunately, for the first couple of years of raising her I had no legal rights to keep Melodi from her mom, so I had to relent and allow Melodi to go with her mama anytime Kelli asked. The thought that, legally, Kelli could take Melodi back any time made me so nervous. I knew that Kelli continued to use drugs and did not have the maturity or stability to properly care for Melodi. Thankfully, Kelli never seriously tried taking back physical custody of Melodi, even though she threatened to do so several times. She eventually did come right out and accuse me once of taking Melodi away from her for selfish motives. She also told Melodi that it was my fault that they were not together and that I prevented her from living with her mama full time without good reason. She filled Melodi with false hope and promises to move Melodi back in with her soon, without making any real changes required to follow through. I lived in fear of Kelli following through with her threat of taking Melodi back at any given time. I worried about the negative influence Kelli had on her daughter while in her care. Kelli remained in a state of denial, continuing to use drugs and maintaining an unhealthy and unsafe lifestyle. I did not want my granddaughter to live in that unsafe and neglectful environment.

Of course, a little girl does not fully understand all of what excellent parenting entails, and for years, Melodi only saw the good in her mama. Common for drug users, Kelli's maturity level lagged years behind her actual age, and even in her mid-twenties, Kelli acted like a silly teenager most of the time. She seemed more like a big sister, rather than a mother, to Melodi. She acted hyper, and played around, like a fun little playmate for Melodi most of the time. Melodi enjoyed it, and she loved going away with her mother. However, it always ended abruptly, so she only saw the lively, good-natured side of her mom. When Kelli tired of it or circumstances soured for her, as they often did, she brought Melodi back to me, usually within six to forty-eight hours, with little explanation to me or her daughter. Complications arose quickly for Kelli, such as a predicament at her job or a conflict with a boyfriend. I never complained about her bringing Melodi home swiftly. I did not feel comfortable with Kelli taking her away, anyway, so I welcomed her back happily.

I faced immense challenges over these issues. The first major challenge was trying to comfort my granddaughter's heartache resulting from her mother and father's rejection and abandonment. Secondly, dealing with the sad irony of my granddaughter resenting me despite all I did for her felt next to impossible. Trying to comfort and counsel my granddaughter who had become somewhat angry and bitter thoroughly tried my patience and left me feeling exhausted, frustrated, heartbroken, and discouraged a great deal of the time. I began to feel overwhelmed. I could not overcome these grim obstacles in and of myself, no matter how hard I tried.

My strong relationship with the Lord kept me moving forward, thankfully. I constantly drew strength from my faith and sought Godly wisdom and direction through prayer and His word, instead of giving in to the despair and hopelessness I felt resulting from Melodi's resentment. I did not know how things could work out positively, but I knew all things were possible for the children of God who remain in Him. I prayed continuously for the Lord to heal my mental grief, and to help me feel nothing but love and compassion for my granddaughter despite her lashing out at me and blaming me for the separation between her and her mother. I cried many nights after tucking her into bed from heartache and mental exhaustion.

I ran out of ideas of how to fix things. I prayed daily to the Lord for comfort, healing, and wisdom. The Bible says in James 1:5 (NIV), "If any of you lacks wisdom, you should ask God, who gives generously to all without finding fault, and it will be given to you." I sought the Lord and reminded Him that I did indeed lack wisdom and requested direction on how to deal with my dilemma. *How do I help a person who resents me? How do I keep from feeling sad and bitter myself, knowing that I rescued this child from an existence of chaos and neglect, yet she blames me for the injustice in her life? How do I love unconditionally?* All the answers were easier said than done! I definitely needed divine intervention.

God answers prayer from a truly humble heart. The merciful Father downloaded advice to me once again. The Lord put a message in my spirit that the time had come to share some brutally honest truths to my granddaughter. Up until that point of Melodi's life, I had been shielding her from the details of her mother's illicit lifestyle. I never spoke about her drug use in front of her. I never mentioned the run-ins she had with the police for breaking laws, such as driving while intoxicated, or possession of drugs, or other crimes and misdemeanors. I did not share my disdain for the many boyfriends that came in and out of her mother's life. I never blamed Kelli for her poor track record with employment in front of my granddaughter and backed up the half-truths she told Melodi about why each boss fired her each time. I wanted little Melodi to grow up with a good self-image, and worried that knowing these bad characteristics of her mother might contribute to feelings of low self-worth. Through Sovereign impartation, though, I believed that the time had come to enlighten her with some difficult truths about her mother, to help her understand the reasons she could not always be with her.

Melodi and I had many serious discussions in the car

during our commute to and from school in the mornings and afternoons. I decided to bring up the issues about her mom during one of our drives. I opened up to my eight-year-old granddaughter on the way home from school one day. I did my best to break down and explain her mom's addictions and problematic lifestyle in the simplest way I could for a young child her age. I also expressed my honest feelings to Melodi about the grief I carried due to the bitterness she directed toward me. I explained that I did not want her to feel guilty, but that I had hurt feelings. I told her that I worked hard to raise her with love and to bless her with a good, safe life, and having her blame me for the problems her mother caused genuinely upset me. I reiterated that I loved her unconditionally and knew that she did not purposefully hurt me. I shared with her my belief that we could achieve full healing and restoration with the Lord's guidance, but we needed to work through these issues, openly and honestly.

I continued my talk with Melodi by telling her that I truly believed her mama had a loving heart and good character. I told her that my daughter made many bad choices, mostly due to selfishness as well as abandoning her relationship with the Lord. I also explained that unfortunately, she had let herself become addicted to drugs which caused major destruction in her life. Knowing the enormous challenge of hearing this news about her mother, I wanted her to know that my heart grieved as well, and she did not suffer alone. I opened up about my passion for my beloved daughter. I told her that it seemed as though my beautiful daughter grew up so quickly, that I absolutely adored her, and that I would never stop loving her no matter what she did. I reminisced about how, as my sweet little baby girl, seemingly not so long ago, I held her almost every waking moment from her birth until she was about eighteen months old, due to an apparent fear of isolation Kelli seemed to have as a baby. She cried incessantly when left alone in her crib, until I picked her up. I told her that I had such high hopes and aspirations about her future, from an early age, due to her beauty, charm, amazing wit, and compassionate personality. I told her how proud it made me to receive so many compliments about her cuteness and charming personality from acquaintances and strangers, as well. I continued by sharing how much I loved the fact that her mama had never met a stranger, made friends so easily, and loved everyone. I told her that her mom had a beautiful soul, and she could not even pass by a homeless person without crying. As a child, when she noticed a homeless person, she asked if she could give them her allowance money, or her pillow from the back of the car during road trips. I lovingly mentioned how during Kelli's childhood, she visited our neighbors daily, forcing me to meet them all because I would not allow her to spend time with people I did not know. I chuckled as I told her that as a little girl, my beloved daughter knew all of our neighbors by name, not to mention the names of all our neighbors' pets and family members, and shared many stories and details with me about these people whom she truly cared about.

I hoped that by opening my heart to Melodi and communicating my true feelings, I could help to grow empathy in her, by showing her she did not grieve alone. I too felt grieved and heartbroken by my daughter's lifestyle and her rejection toward me. As a mother and now a grandmother, I often tried to shield my children from pain by hiding my "bad feelings", like sadness, anger, or rejection, thinking they could not handle seeing me distressed. I thought I was helping them by only showing them a positive, strong side of myself. I began to realize that this misconception likely only caused me to seem cold or distant to them. We all make mistakes. We all suffered during trials of life. Trying to pretend otherwise did not foster close, loving relationships. I knew I had some changes I needed to make too.

After I shared my heart with Melodi, explaining my own feelings of disappointment and rejection, I shared the hope I had as well. I told Melodi that Jesus could save her mom and deliver her from this dangerous, drug-addicted lifestyle, and how I totally believed that He would. I shared in raw honesty that, yes, I had a broken heart, and cried many tears on account of her mama's hazardous lifestyle, but that I also had a promise from God of her restoration. I received a prophecy, a message from God Himself, spoken to me through the pastor of our church, Greg Thurstonson, during a Sunday church service.

Pastor Greg Thurstonson spoke directly to me and gave me a life-changing prophecy. I shared the whole miraculous account with Melodi. One Saturday afternoon a year or so prior, I felt extremely defeated and heartbroken thinking about Kelli's life and struggles with drug dependence. Wanting some solitude, I went into my bedroom, locked myself in the restroom, and cried. I wept bitterly. I felt hopeless and devastated after years of dealing with an addict that I could not help or change. I cried and prayed to the Lord for over an hour in desperation. I knew

I could count on my husband anytime I needed him, but that particular day, I just cried by myself and prayed to God. After a while, although still feeling overwhelmed with sadness, I wiped my tears away, pretended everything was okay, and continued my daily routines. I never said anything to my husband or family that day, but chose to suffer alone, trying to deal with my feelings of despair by myself.

The next morning, we attended the service at Dominion Church, as usual, an Assembly of God, Spirit-filled church in League City, Texas. I always enjoyed the praise and worship portion of the service at the beginning. The worship pastor, Deena Thurstonson, along with other singers and a band, performed four or five energetic and uplifting songs, while the congregation stood and sang along. I will never forget that special morning, as the Lord chose to speak to me through His prophet, our pastor, Greg Thurstonson. While I stood in front of my seat, singing with the congregation, Pastor Greg came into the sanctuary from the back of the room, on the same side as my husband and me. He stopped at our row and told Aaron and me he needed to talk to us right then and there while the music and singing continued. He gently pulled us over to the aisle to "huddle up" with my husband and me to speak with us, semi-privately. He spoke loudly as this "meeting" began right in the middle of the praise and worship service. He told us that the Lord had placed my husband and me on his heart yesterday very strongly. He said that he knew we faced a huge struggle with our daughter and that the Lord saw our immense pain. Then he continued by speaking directly to me, and to the best of my recollection, said,

"Julia, I particularly want to talk to you as a mama who is hurting very badly. God says that He sees your mama's heart and how much you love and cry for your daughter and your children. God wants me to tell you that He loves the broken-hearted and He wants to heal your broken heart. I felt this so strongly, Julia, that I almost called you yesterday. In fact, the Lord told me to call you yesterday, but I'm sorry, I did not. He wants me to tell you that He sees your pain, that He loves you and you can ask Him for anything, and He will give it to you, His daughter. He also says that you can rest in the comfort of His promise to you that all of your children will be saved. I just felt this message so strongly yesterday, and I'm sorry that I waited until today, but I had to tell you this right now, Julia." Then he hugged Aaron and me and walked up to his seat toward the front of the sanctuary.

Talk about an amazing event! That special moment and those words given to me by my pastor touched my heart deeply and truly changed my life and my outlook about the future. To know that the God of the universe saw me in my little bathroom in my house, crying in distress, and heard every word I desperately prayed to Him meant the world to me. To think, I touched the heart of the Lord enough to have our pastor give me that message straight from Him. I have received many messages of encouragement from the Bible, the inspired Word of God, throughout my life, but God knew I needed something more at that time. I cherish that astonishing experience, where an actual person, a minister of God, who barely knew me and had no knowledge of me crying out for help the day before, gave me a direct message from the Lord above. My faith grew immensely from that incredibly miraculous experience.

It felt good sharing the prophetic, faith-building Word I received from our pastor with Melodi. While being brutally honest with her about the treacherous path her mother chose to live at that time, I wanted to instill the hope I had into her, as well. The Lord prompted me to tell her the whole truth about her mother's issues at that time, so we could deal with our feelings, and face them honestly. I told her that I completely believed in total restoration and healing for her mama. I empathized with the new challenge Melodi faced of discovering the magnitude of problems and inner struggles her mother had, but I knew she had to find out sooner or later. God impressed in me that Melodi should know the truth.

I also hoped that when Melodi heard the details about her mom's unscrupulous lifestyle, she could understand the reasons why she lived with me, and recognize that we wanted nothing but the best life for her. It hurt deeply to have my precious granddaughter regard me negatively. I hoped things would change between us for the better now that she knew more of the truth. I believed in faith that my daughter would come to her senses one day, and that she would get off the drugs and live a healthy, sober life. My heart and soul grew weary as I watched my beautiful daughter essentially killing herself using drugs and risking her life almost every day from the effects of her drug addiction, but I never lost my faith. I came very close to losing faith a couple of times, and hung onto it by a thread, but never completely forsook my belief in her future healing. My pastor often quoted the scripture from Proverbs 13:12 (NKJV), "Hope deferred makes the heart

grow weary, but when the desire comes, it is a tree of life."
How long could my deferred hope last? I wondered. The
pain felt unbearable at times. I clung to that beautiful
scripture verse from Proverbs and longed for the "tree of
life" to come to pass. My pastor spoke that particular scripture to the congregation at the end of several sermons and
often invited people to come to the altar for prayer. He
sympathized with those of us in the congregation hurting
from unanswered prayer and had elders of the church come
and pray for those of us with broken hearts. Spending time
with God at the church altar and having another person pray
over me kept me grounded in sanity and strong faith.
Church community blessed me through life's struggles
again and again.

Melodi seemed to handle the cold, hard truth I gave her
about her mother pretty well. I think she appreciated my
honesty with her and had more respect for what I was going
through. The talk we had helped our relationship and I saw
maturity and empathy toward me from Melodi start to grow
as time went on.

The Lord continued to humble my heart, and I did not
hide the struggles I had with my daughter from others. I did
not want pride or embarrassment to keep me from receiving
love and comfort from my friends, family, and church community. Thankfully, the Lord revealed to me that hiding the
cause of my pain and suffering from others would only
prolong the travail. This tactic of pride, shame, and hiding
our true feelings from our loved ones comes from the
enemy of our soul, the devil, with the goal of keeping us
isolated from other humans. At that time, I had a very good
friend and coworker with a son suffering from drug

addictions. When she and I discussed Kelli's problems, she shared her own similar feelings of mental stress and pain due to her son's drug use and the way his life had spiraled out of control. We talked a lot, but she always asked me not to share anything we talked about with anyone else. She explained that she felt so alone, but she did not want to reach out for help from anyone about her son's problems because of her "position in the community". She said that the negative stigma attached to having a child with a drug addiction would hurt her standing in the community. What people thought of her and her family was very important to her. I assured her that I would never reveal her business to anyone else. I felt sorry for her for believing it necessary to keep her pain bottled up most of the time. I did not just go around telling everyone about my daughter and her addictions, but many times I felt free to open up and share my heart, humbly and honestly. It comforted me to have friends on whom I could call during low times, or a new prayer warrior to enlist for support, without letting pride stand in my way or isolate me.

I cherished the tremendous overwhelming support bestowed on me due to my vulnerability and honesty. I loved the liberation I felt from not having to hide or be ashamed of my daughter's struggles. The process of surrendering my pride began shortly after I gave my heart to the Lord as a young adult. The favor and acceptance I experienced from showing my imperfections far outweighed any sense of superiority I may have attained by faking a flawless persona. I enjoyed more respect and esteem as a candid, unpretentious person, than I had in my past, when I attempted to conceal my faults and keep skeletons tucked away in the closet. I believe the devil uses pride and fear as two of his best tactics to keep people isolated from others.

One of the first steps to getting help with life's burdens usually involves the cathartic act of sharing our heartaches and difficulties with others. Your friends and family can be helpful allies as they provide a supportive shoulder for you. They may counsel you and pray for you, or just listen as you share your heart. For all you know, your friend may have struggled through a similar situation, and may have ideas about how to deal with a difficult circumstance that you face. If nothing else, your openness and vulnerability can bring compassion and favor from others. I experienced that quite frequently once I surrendered my pride. I never felt judgement on account of the struggles that my daughter or I had. If anyone ever looked down on me, I considered that none of my business.

Still, hope deferred makes a heart sick. My deferred hope lasted a very long while. *Why did I have to agonize through this extensive trial*, I wondered at times. But, more appropriately, I thought, *why did my daughter have to suffer all those years*? I had always heard that addicts have to hit "rock bottom" before finally realizing they need to turn their life around and get help to stop abusing drugs. Kelli had already committed so many atrocious acts and suffered so many negative consequences from them, that it seemed "rock bottom" kept sinking lower and lower. My family and I wondered when Kelli would ever reach the preverbal "rock bottom". *How low could it descend?* This girl remained a stubborn, die-hard drug user no matter what happened. Her life cycled through a series of ups and downs, mostly downs, and back again. She made new friends and lost them within weeks. She constantly engaged in altercations with people. She got evicted from apartments often and frequently had to relocate. She got hired and then fired at jobs within a few days. More tragically, she became pregnant out of wedlock three times, with three different fathers. She had encounters with the law, both as a victim, as well as a criminal. She served time in jail for committing grand theft auto. She got arrested for driving under the influence of an intoxicating substance a couple of times. She even suffered a terrible car accident when driving while intoxicated, where the car rolled over twice, and incredibly survived with very few injuries. Once, some of her so-called "friends" locked her in a car and set it on fire. Thank God she escaped. *How did this girl go through so much, yet continue in this precarious lifestyle?*

I held onto my faith in God for dear life and continued to believe for my daughter's deliverance. I prayed and claimed the promises of God and asked others to pray for us often. Many times the enemy of my soul whispered discouraging thoughts to me, telling me praying did no good, or that people grew tired of praying for me and my daughter, but I did not listen to those lies. I knew the importance and effectiveness of prayer. I believed the verse in the Bible in James 5:16 (NKJV), "The effective fervent prayer of a righteous man avails much." The Bible even talks about our prayers when describing a scene in Heaven in the book of Revelation. Chapter 5 talks about "twenty-four elders that are surrounding the Lord at the throne, who are holding golden bowls full of incense, which are the prayers of the saints". I have confidence that God finds our prayers precious, and they do not fall on deaf ears. What a beautiful picture Revelation describes of God storing our prayers in golden bowls! I do not always know how, but I know God can do all things, and I believe the whole written Word of God in the Holy Bible, and I live for the hope I gain by trusting in the promises of God.

God speaks to His servants in many different ways. God knows our needs and will do anything it takes to reach us. The Word says He rewards those who diligently seek Him. God spoke to my husband and me and directed us to make a very important change that we desperately needed. One day, I heard a message from God directly in my spirit. Then, upon request, the Lord even confirmed His words to me through my husband.

On a Sunday morning, the day I heard God speak to me, I felt sad and upset. I do not remember the particular reason for my sorrow, but I sought the Lord for comfort once again. Prior to joining Dominion Church, we belonged to another local body of believers. We attended the service there that Sunday morning. At the end of the service, the pastor asked if anybody in the congregation would like to come up to the altar for prayer. Many evangelical churches have a time of prayer in the altars at some point during their services. That morning, I had a strong desire to have some-one pray for me, so I approached one of the church leaders at the altar. I told him that I felt extremely sad about my daughter Kelli, and that I would appreciate prayer for faith and comfort. I also requested that he pray for healing for my daughter. This man and I knew each other very well. As a friend of our family, he already knew Kelli's whole story, and her many life struggles, including her problem with addictions. He had counseled and prayed for me and my family many times prior to that day. He also knew Kelli personally, as she had attended that church with our family for years as a child and into her teenage years. Directly after I gave the gentleman my prayer request, unexpectedly, I heard the voice of God say to my spirit, "This man has grown weary of praying for you and your daughter Kelli. You do not belong at this church anymore." These specific words surprised me, as I did not feel any negativity about the man I asked to pray for me, and nothing had happened to lead me to believe he had grown tired of praying for Kelli and me. I look back now and thank God for that revelation. The Lord did not want me in a church that did not feed me spiritually. I did not realize it then, but my relationship with the Lord had grown stagnant at that place of worship. My Father gave me something very important to think about. *Should I continue to attend that church solely out of loyalty to the pastor and congregation? Did that church help me continue to grow spiritually, or did I maintain my attendance there because it felt comfortable?* I had been a member of that church for over twenty years!

The message I clearly heard the Lord speak in my heart gave me a lot to think about. I did not expect to hear something like that at all. I loved my church and had been attending services there several times a week for years. I had no thoughts or intentions of leaving it. After becoming pregnant as an unwed teenager, my sister Margie helped me receive salvation through Jesus Christ and invited me to that church. I became a member within the first year I started attending. My children went to that church and "grew up" with that congregation. I sang on the praise team, met my husband there, and had many close friends who also attended there. Hearing the Lord speak that unexpected message to my heart really made me wonder about some things. I thought about the gentleman from whom I requested prayer. I considered his character and felt no animosity toward him. I never spoke to him about what I heard from the Lord that morning. Perhaps it had become difficult for him to continue to pray for a specific need for years and years, and not see any apparent improvement in the situation. I did not blame him for having imperfect faith. We are all imperfect and lose our faith sometimes. I know I had let my faith slip many times.

I remember sensing the words of the Lord in my spirit so clearly that morning, "… you do not belong at this church anymore". I trusted the Lord, and often reminded myself of the scripture in Romans 8:28 (NKJV) that says, "All things work together for good to those who love God, to those who are called according to His purpose." I definitely wanted to seek the Lord's wisdom. I prayed to God, "Dear Lord, I heard a message from You, deep in my spirit, telling me that the man I asked to pray for me, one of the leaders of the church, had lost the desire to pray for me. I also believe I heard you tell me that I do not belong at that church anymore. I believe that You spoke that message to me, Lord. I will do whatever You ask of me, Father, because I completely trust You. However, I deeply desire to confirm that You spoke those words to me, Lord, before I act on them. I had no plans of leaving my church, so please help me to know for sure whether I heard Your voice or not. Lord, if You are truly leading my family and me to find another church to attend, please confirm this to me through my husband, without me telling him what I heard this morning at the altar. In Jesus' name I pray. Thank you, Lord. Amen."

The good Lord answered my prayer. A few days later, my husband and I sat together alone at the dinner table. After our meal, we talked about some of the events from that week, and the topic of our church came up in the conversation. My husband brought up the subject, and we talked a little bit about the service from the previous Sunday. I purposefully did not mention anything about the Lord's message to me or even talk about our church all week. So, what my husband said next seemed to come out of the clear blue sky, "You know what, Julia?" my husband asked, "For some reason, I just do not feel like we belong at that church anymore." My husband told me later that he did not have any particular reason for making that statement, and he kind of just said it as a whim, but his words instantly provided the confirmation that I needed. I immediately told Aaron that the Lord had communicated the very same point to me in church that last Sunday, with those very same words, "you do not belong at this church anymore". I also told him that I had asked God if He could please confirm the message through my husband. We both felt amazed and happy that God still spoke to His children, and we agreed to trust the Lord and answer His call. We made plans to start looking for another church right away, confident in the Lord's leading.

4

God Speaks and Leads

MY husband and I made plans to visit different churches in our area to find another one we liked. We thought it would be wise to visit a new church three times before deciding to join, in order to fairly gage the atmosphere of each potential new church.

We decided to visit Dominion Church first. Aaron and I had heard their youth pastor, Clint DeGroot, preach and the Dominion Church youth band perform when they came as a guest speaker and guest worship band at our church a few weeks prior. We thoroughly enjoyed them! As music connoisseurs, my husband and I loved the visiting youth group's band and their style of worship music they played during the service. We felt extremely impressed with the young lady who played the bass in the church band. She stood out from the rest of the youth, with her unique physical appearance and charismatic spirit, while she played the bass guitar. She wore a rocker-style outfit and had jet-black, spiked hair. She reminded my husband and me of our middle daughter, Tiffani, and seemed about her same age. Tiffani also loved to play the guitar and dressed in a similar "rocker girl" fashion. Tiffani, however, had strayed away from her relationship with the Lord. Our prodigal daughter who once had a close relationship with God, turned away from Him, and now suffered from depression. My husband and I longed for a close relationship with Tiffani, but could not get her to open up and share her feelings with us anymore. We longed to see that same joyfulness in our daughter Tiffani that we noticed in the energetic young lady playing the bass guitar for the Dominion Church youth group. We later found out that the young lady was Morgan Thurstonson, one of the daughters of the Senior Pastors, Greg and Deena Thurstonson, from Dominion Church.

We also appreciated the preaching of Clint deGroot, the guest youth pastor from Dominion Church that spoke at our old church a few weeks prior to that day, as well. His loving and humble spirit stood out during his preaching. He spoke about the Lord with genuine zeal and sincerity. He showed great compassion and sensitivity for the lost souls of the younger generation and even wept during his sermon. We enjoyed his down-to-earth personality and laughed out loud at the stories of his self-proclaimed awkwardness he shared. My husband and I are drawn to and appreciate that style of preaching, those who exhibit sincerity, unpretentiousness, compassion, candid humor, and humility through their speaking.

Aaron and I prepared to search for nothing less than a friendly, top-quality church that fit all of the expectations on our list. We wanted to remain in the Assembly of God church denomination. My husband and I agreed in the high importance of finding a church with an excellent music ministry and praise team, as well as honest pastors who preach the Word of God with unwavering faith in the Bible. We also looked for a church with exceptional programs for children and youth. We really hated leaving our church because we met and fell in love with each other there, but we truly felt that the Lord had spoken to us, and we drew inspiration from God's holy impartation. We both also felt a sense of weariness from the trials we had been struggling through over the past several years and hoped for a fresh start in our walks with the Lord.

The next Sunday we attended our first prospective new congregation, Dominion Church, located in our hometown of League City, Texas, on Landing Boulevard. We attended only one Sunday service at Dominion Church and became "hooked"! So much for our plans to attend several different places of worship and stay at each one as guests for three weeks. We immediately fell in love with everything about Dominion Church and did not want to go anywhere else.

A healing process began in me immediately when we started attending Dominion Church. The praise and worship services at our new church played a huge part in my healing. I loved the lively song choices played and sung by the worship band and the praise team. The dynamic worship leader, the pastor's wife, had a beautiful singing voice, and invited the congregation to stand and sing along by their seats or in the altars at the front of the sanctuary. A giant screen on the wall displayed the words to the inspirational, contemporary Christian songs. I felt joy coming back to my spirit for the first time in a long while as I sang along and worshipped the Lord.

From our first visit to Dominion Church, I felt very comfortable and safe there. During praise and worship, after about three songs, the worship leader quieted the music down and invited members from the congregation up to the front to receive prayer, if needed. I left my seat and joined several others who gathered at the front for prayer. An usher directed me to join an older couple who stood by the altars as part of the prayer team. John and Mary Fowler welcomed me with smiles and outstretched hands as I walked toward them. They asked me for my prayer request, and I told them briefly about my grown daughter who suffered from drug addictions. I also shared about my discouragement and weariness from facing years of spiritual and physical battles as well as my desire for encouragement and renewed faith.

I sensed God doing a fresh work in me instantly as the sweet-natured, caring couple, John and Mary Fowler, prayed for me that morning, during our first visit to Dominion Church. The three of us joined hands in a circle and prayed. I felt renewed in my spirit and loved by God. I do not recall their exact prayer, but I remember feeling their genuine compassion as Mrs. Fowler took my hand and prayed for me and my daughter Kelli. It brought me to tears. I thanked the Lord that He led my husband and me to that church by speaking to our spirit. I began to feel a new love and compassion that I did not realize had been slowly fading away. Our Father works in very mysterious ways. He only wants the best for His children and we can completely trust Him to guide us in all areas of our lives.

Some folks may wonder how I could share such deep personal downfalls about my life and my daughter's life with complete strangers without shame or fear of judgement. Some might even disagree with my doing so, but I believe the benefits of trusting others, sometimes blindly, far outweigh the risks. First of all, my desperation for help became my top priority, reason number one, for sharing my story with people I had just met in the altar at a new church. I knew I needed more help to deal with the overwhelming pain I endured for years and could not continue to survive alone. In addition to the love and encouragement from my husband and family, I desired a bigger network of supporters to get through the anguish I experienced.

My second reason for sharing my story at the altar with new people arose from a desire for Godly counsel. I trusted the Lord to guide me to people who could help me with scripture, prayer, and encouragement, to give me hope for a better future for my daughter. I realized not everyone could be trusted, but I never felt forsaken by God because He had already brought me so far during this battle. Nobody is perfect. I definitely knew that. I once became betrayed by a Christian friend through a massive deception scheme, which surprised me and caught me off guard, but my Father always provided me with reasons to hang on. I knew not to blame God for the fault of a fallen sister in the Lord because we all have a free will to do whatever we want. I felt His peace during times of prayer, and He directed me to certain scriptures in the Bible through His Holy Spirit. I did not have perfect faith, but I sought Him diligently, and He gave me wisdom and direction. Many times, the Lord guides and comforts me by speaking directly to my spirit, and at other times, I receive advice and help through Christian fellowship.

The third reason I chose to have such candidness with strangers results from the act of being surrendered to God. I could not afford to hold on to vanity anymore due to such painful experiences in life. I stopped worrying about whether or not people thought I had a perfect life or impeccable children. I did not have a flawless life, nor did anybody else. I knew admitting to others that I had a daughter addicted to drugs could bring reproach from some people, but I refused to wear a mask that attempted to hide faults and failures anymore. I did not care who knew any longer. I love fellow unpretentious humans. Each person I met became a potential prayer partner to me, in my mind. I would accept help anywhere I could get it.

Over the next couple of months, as we continued attending Dominion, a healing process beautifully blossomed in me. Our plans to visit other churches never happened. We found our home church, and we loved it. We felt like family, listening to senior pastor Greg Thurstonson's sermons, delivered with humor and vulnerability. I never went to a counselor or attended group therapy, but definitely found healing in another way. Or, actually, I believe healing found me. I began to realize soon after we started attending Dominion, that I had been experiencing a mild depression that I needed to deal with. I considered going to counseling many times, as I know it provides helpful and often necessary mental health growth, but I just never fit it into my schedule. But, interestingly, the Lord began healing me through prayer and the praise and worship service at our new church. All of the sadness that I neglected to deal with properly over the years suddenly began to come to the surface at that time. After that first Sunday when I received prayer from John and Mary Fowler, I felt renewed hope. All the bouts of depression I had experienced throughout my life came upon me so slowly and subtly, that I did not realize I was depressed until a few months after its onset. The depression caused a numbness in my emotional state, and I pushed the sad and uncomfortable feelings aside as a coping mechanism. I am so thankful to God for leading me to a new house of worship. Miraculously, during every praise and worship service on Sunday mornings, instead of feeling depressed, I felt pure joy. Every song sung and word spoken by our worship leader went straight to my heart in complete happiness. But then, unfortunately, the cloud of depression returned on Monday morning, and stayed with me until the next Sunday when I returned to church. I really struggled to mentally make it through each week. I craved to feel the peace and joy that I literally only experienced on Sunday mornings during praise and worship at Dominion Church.

For about six to eight weeks I continued this unique pattern of feeling depressed all week from Monday through Saturday, and then experiencing pure joy in the song service on Sunday. I continued to drag myself through the week in a state of melancholy, and then went to church on Sunday morning and felt blissful elation. God began a work in me, though. As strange as it may sound, my literal healing occurred through praise and worship music. I do not know how He did it, but after a couple of months of this cycle, I became completely healed from depression. Thank God! Amazingly, my mind and spirit were completely healed. This reaffirmed my belief that God truly does work in mysterious ways.

We continued to attend Dominion Church and joined the congregation. After about a year of attending Dominion, the pastor asked me to join the praise and worship team as a singer. I did not hesitate to accept his offer because I love to minister in song. I have a long, enjoyable history of singing in choirs throughout my whole life since I was in the sixth-grade school choir. I also sang in the choirs in junior high, high school, and even in junior college, as well as on the praise team at every church to which I belonged. I just love singing, and I will sing as part of the congregation, as a member of the praise team, or even with just an audience of One, the Lord Himself. I have to sing. Singing gives me life! I love attending a Spirit-filled church, with the freedom to worship in any preferred style. We can worship God by singing loudly or softly, lifting our hands, dancing, sitting or jumping, kneeling, or even through tears. As the Word says in 2 Corinthians 3:17 (NIV), "Now the Lord is the Spirit, and where the Spirit of the Lord is, there is freedom." That freedom in the Lord to sing and worship in any and all ways is so refreshing, life-giving, and healing to my spirit.

Meanwhile, unfortunately, my daughter continued to struggle with drug addiction, and I continued raising my granddaughter. I critically needed to keep my faith in God, if only for the sake of my sanity, regardless of the circumstances of Kelli's life. After my healing from depression, my faith grew in leaps and bounds. I learned so much about myself. I completely forgave myself for all my imperfections and past failures and began trying to see myself as God sees me, forgiven, unique, and loveable. When tempted to think bad thoughts about myself or label myself with degrading words, I immediately erased those thoughts from my head, recognizing the ploys of the enemy. Instead, I read Bible scriptures, prayed, and intentionally filled my mind with positive thoughts. I reminded myself of how I raised my children marvelously as a fantastic mother, doing the best I could. I adopted this scripture as a motto for my life, from Philippians 4:8-9 (KJV), "Finally, brethren, whatsoever things are true, whatsoever things are honest, whatsoever things are just, whatsoever things are pure, whatsoever things are lovely, whatsoever things are of good report; if there be any virtue, and if there be any praise, think on these things. …and the God of peace shall be with you."

When my children were young, I talked with them often about the Lord and taught them stories from the Bible, and I did this with my granddaughter Melodi also. Each week, I asked them about the lesson from children's church. If they had any questions about a Bible lesson, I explained more about it for clarification and conversation. We discussed God and the Bible at the dinner table often in our family because of our passion for the things of God, and our belief in the truth of the whole Bible and its teachings. At the age of six years old, I told Melodi about the process of receiving salvation through Jesus Christ. I assumed that she had already heard about it many times in church, as we attended twice a week, but I felt a duty to discuss it with her, as her mother figure, and make sure she understood it completely.

I explained the salvation story to Melodi basically the same way I had told her mother and my other two children at that approximate age, when I felt they could understand the basic concept. I shared this information, in a basic manner, with each of my beloved children and grand-daughter, saying in effect, "Jesus is God's son and was born as a human to take away the sins of all of the people in the world. He never sinned or did anything wrong. He lived His life helping people and healing them of sicknesses and diseases. He spent His whole life spreading love and telling people about God, His father in Heaven. When He grew up, He was killed and hung on a cross. He died for our sins. On the third day, after His death, He came back to life. He told everyone that if they repent of their sins and accept Him into their heart and live for Him, they are saved. If we do that, we will go to Heaven and live forever there with Him, and we do not have to go to Hell when we die." I always tried to make the account of salvation very basic and age appropriate for my children, and did this for Melodi, as well. All three of my children listened intently, accepted these truths, and asked me to help them pray to receive Jesus into their hearts.

When I explained Christian salvation to Melodi, she had a rather different and impactful reaction to it than my children or anybody else I knew ever did. Melodi sat and listened very intently and considerately as I gave her the basic details and knowledge of how to become a Christian. After I finished, she asked, "What is Hell? What happens if you have to go there?" What an honest and innocent question!

I answered honestly, "Hell is the place down below with fire, where the devil lives. If you do not accept Jesus as your Savior, you go there when you die, and live in the fire forever."

Melodi took this information straight to her heart, and instantly started crying hysterically! "What?" she cried, "Why would you have to go to a place with fire? That's terrible!" She continued bawling and crying in anguish and disbelief. Her shocked reaction took me aback. I portrayed the steps to salvation similarly to my three children and a few other people in the past, and none of them reacted with such shock and horror. I have to assume none of them took the description of Hell so literally, or perhaps they did not concentrate on the impending doom of Hell as seriously as Melodi. I do believe the Bible's description of Hell as a literal place, and that people actually go there after death, unfortunately, if they do not believe on Jesus Christ as their Savior. However, I never witnessed anyone cry out so dreadfully when told about it.

Melodi kept crying, and I sat there with her in silence for a couple of minutes. I did not know what to do at first. Her reaction took me by surprise. I felt awful! I hated seeing her so distraught, and questioned my decision to include the explanation of Hell while teaching her about salvation. I hoped to console her. "Melodi, it's okay, sweetie! We don't have to go to Hell. That's why Jesus died for us. If we pray and ask Him into our heart, we will be saved, and we don't have to go down there."

"But that's so mean," she cried, "I can't believe anyone would have to live in fire forever!"

"I know it sounds terrible, Melodi," I said, "but nobody has to go there. Jesus died for everyone." I reiterated, "Every single person that was ever born in this world has the opportunity to get saved through Jesus Christ. Then they get to go to Heaven when they die. But each person has a choice as to whether they want to believe in Jesus or not."

Then Melodi asked, "But what about the people who never hear about Jesus? Or what about little kids who die before they can even talk or understand words?"

Melodi, while still visibly very upset, asked very intelligent questions. I further explained my convictions to her, "Well, I believe in my heart, Melodi, that every person somehow, some way, gets a chance to hear about salvation through Jesus dying for all people. Maybe they hear it through another person, maybe they read it in the Bible, or perhaps God reveals it to them in their heart and soul, miraculously. The Bible says that God can even speak to people through a dream or vision. And if a child dies, or someone without the mental capability to understand the salvation message, then, I believe, they automatically go to Heaven after their death. The Bible talks about a person having to reach a certain age before they are responsible or held accountable for their soul."

She further questioned, "But what if there are people in places on the earth that never hear about Jesus? That's not fair for them to have to go to Hell!"

I completely understood Melodi's question, as I had asked that same question at one time in my life. I answered, "Your questions make a lot of sense, Melodi. Through many years of living as a Christian, studying the Bible, and asking the Lord for wisdom, I have faith that every person that ever exists, now or in the past, somehow gets the chance to give their heart to the Lord. I really believe that God is big enough to make that possible," I continued. "And, like I said, I truly believe that if someone dies as a child or if they are mentally challenged and cannot understand the concept of salvation," I explained again, "they will get to be with Jesus when they die, as well. I have known God for a long time. He is fair and He loves justice. The Bible says that Jesus died for the sins of all people, but every person must make the choice for him or herself. We all get to choose if we want to live for Jesus and receive salvation or not."

Melodi began to calm down after I explained salvation through Jesus, Heaven, and Hell more thoroughly. We talked a little bit more about the subject, and I restated that she gets to make her own choice about what she believes. I reassured her that if she ever wanted to pray and ask Jesus into her heart, that I would be happy to lead her in that prayer anytime. Later that same day at bedtime, while I sat at her bedside, she expressed her desire to pray and ask Jesus to come into her heart as her Savior. Overflowing with joy, I agreed to help her pray. We closed our eyes and joined hands, and I told her to repeat this prayer, "Dear Jesus, I know that all people are born as sinners in this world and that I am a sinner. I know that You are God's son, Jesus, and that you died for my sins. I am sorry for all my sins and I ask that You come into my heart as my Savior. Please help me to live for You for the rest of my life. In Jesus' name I pray, amen." We talked about God's abundant love for her and how He felt so happy she made the decision to become a Christian. I told her how all of the angels in Heaven sang with joy because she chose to become a born-again child of God. My heart and spirit soared with gladness knowing my granddaughter chose to receive Jesus into her heart and soul.

Melodi really did experience a conversion, not just in her soul, but in her personality, as well, after praying to God for forgiveness and salvation. As a toddler up until then, she almost always had a slightly gloomy countenance. She looked melancholy in most of her school pictures. Her eyes did not have a bright sparkle, but more of a sadness, as though missing something. After that day we prayed, I noticed great changes in her. She began to open up and share her feelings more freely. She did not seem so serious and somber anymore. I saw Melodi's personality blossom with confidence, joyfulness, and a lighthearted demeanor. She loved her classes at our church, and she adored the children's church pastors, Kacey and Aaron Martinez. She made many friends in her classes, both at school and at church. She enjoyed playing with her friends and talked about them a lot. I felt so proud because I started seeing her express her newfound joy and excitement about her relationship with the Lord to her friends at church and school.

About a year and a half after Melodi's salvation, the children's pastor planned to have water baptisms for children in our church who had given their hearts to the Lord. I asked Melodi if she wanted to get baptized in water. I explained the significance of water baptism, to make sure she knew exactly what it meant. Before the baptism ceremony, the church held an informational class for the interested parents and children. Melodi felt confident in her decision to get baptized, so we signed her up for the class. Pastors Kacey and Aaron told the students all about baptism and explained the process to them. They asked the parents to have a discussion with their child to clarify all of the information, and verify their resolution. Melodi felt sheer excitement about the upcoming baptism, although she felt some nervousness, too.

We invited all of our family to Melodi's baptism, which would be held during one of our Sunday morning services at Dominion Church. Many members of our family joined us. Our large, extended family filled up two rows of pews in the sanctuary that blessed morning of the baptism service. My husband and I felt so honored to have our family join us for the occasion. Many came from different church denominations, and a few came who did not attend church at all, except on rare occasion. I hoped and prayed that my family and other visitors to our church felt welcome and would experience a special touch from the Lord at the service.

My heart filled with gratitude as I thought about Melodi's teachers and friends from Dominion Church, and how much they helped her over the last few years. Melodi requested to have her pastor, Mrs. Kacey Martinez, baptize her. Pastor Kacey meant the world to Melodi! She never hesitated to help Melodi throughout the many trials and heartaches she experienced. Melodi showed extreme maturity and humbleness when asking others to pray for her mom and bravely articulated her needs with others. She felt safe enough to openly admit that, at times, sadness overwhelmed her, due to the fact that her mother abused drugs. She even confided in her close friends and teachers while her mom served time in jail, and asked for prayer and consolation from her broken heart. Thankfully, no one ever teased or belittled her about her mother's issues. Pastors Aaron and Kacey and others in the church not only prayed with her, but they also took time to counsel with her, and went above and beyond duty to show her love and kindness.

The day before Melodi's baptism service, the church called to inform me that, due to a change of plans, the church's senior pastor intended to perform the baptisms instead of Pastor Kacey. Pastor Kacey would not be able to attend church due to an unforeseen conflict. Although Melodi loved our senior pastor, this news upset her very much. She looked forward to Pastor Kacey baptizing her due to their special relationship. I sent a message to Pastor Kacey and told her about Melodi's disappointment about the change of plans, but explained that we understood. I complimented her on the wonderful job she did as Melodi's pastor. I told her how much she meant to Melodi and thanked her for her unconditional love and kindness toward Melodi throughout the years.

That night, Melodi and I talked about the baptism scheduled for the next day. She said she felt a bit hesitant about it and wondered why Pastor Kacey could not attend. I told her to try not to worry, and that her Papa Aaron and I felt so proud of her decision to become a Christian and get baptized in water. I reminded her that she knew and loved Pastor Greg, the one who would baptize her the next day, and reminisced with her about how she used to call him "Pastor Funny Guy" when we first started attending the church. She laughed at his funny antics and the crazy stories he told during his sermons when she sat with us during church services. She felt better thinking about "Pastor Funny Guy", but still had a slight reservation about the next day. None the less, she agreed to go ahead with the baptism.

The next day, we sat in the church sanctuary with our family waiting for Melodi's baptism, filled with happiness. Then, we found out some great news. Due to hearing about Melodi's disappointment, Pastor Kacey made a special effort to change her plans, just so that she could come to church and baptize Melodi after all. Melodi's wish came true! Kacey told me that morning that it touched her heart deeply when she heard about how strongly Melodi hoped to be baptized by her. She felt so moved, that it compelled her to rearrange her schedule for Melodi and perform her baptism that morning. Pastor Kacey's gesture meant so much to Melodi and me! The blessed event, Melodi's water baptism ceremony, turned out beautifully, with our sweet family group by our side.

5

The Struggles of an Addict

KELLI'S drama continued. So many issues! So much drama! She struggled keeping a job. With her wit and charming personality, she always found new employment easily, but could never keep the job for any amount of time. Pretty much everyone meeting Kelli at first automatically fell in love with her personality. She came across as one who totally had her life together. Managers usually hired her on the spot. Then, after only a few days or a week or two, various problems arose, and she usually became terminated within a couple of months.

We saw the same inconsistency with Kelli in her relationships, such as, with a new boyfriend or between friends. It seemed that every time Kelli came over to pick up Melodi for a visit, she had a new boyfriend. My husband and I tried to have an open mind when she brought a new boyfriend to our home. We acted friendly and usually invited the young man into our house, if he came to the door with Kelli. Many of them just waited in the car for Kelli, though. From what my husband and I believed, not coming to the door of your girlfriend's parent's house seemed to show that the lad did not have a lot of respect for Kelli or her family. Either he lacked respect, or he did not take his relationship with our daughter very seriously. Not a good way to start out, in our opinion.

Kelli always struggled financially, too. Although capable of much more, her education stopped at the high school level. At least, she did complete online classes to attain a GED degree a couple of years after dropping out of high school. With no college degree, her choices for employment only included low paying jobs, mostly in the fast-food industry. Employers usually saw the potential in Kelli, due to her intelligence, personality, and leadership skills, and often offered her a promotion. However, her addictive personality caused aggression or moodiness at times. She often lashed out at coworkers, customers, or even her bosses if something did not go her way. When she relayed the information to me about these incidents, she never held herself accountable. She always blamed others for all the arguments she got into with coworkers or downplayed them by calling them "misunderstandings". Or, better yet, she often had this to say to me after losing a job, "Mom, I'm so mad! I got fired from this place for no reason whatsoever!" Then, upon further inquiry, she usually confessed additional details about the situation, leading me to piece together more from the story, including her main part in the problem. Then, I could tell it was not just a one-sided act of unfairness like she claimed. It did not take a rocket scientist to unravel her fabrications, and I saw the destructive road on which she traveled.

Like many addicts, Kelli had several run-ins with the

police. They arrested her for several minor charges as well as for a couple of more serious offenses. She earned time in jail a few times, serving two or three days, and even landed in prison twice, serving longer sentences. The first time she got arrested, she called me and asked me to come bail her out of jail. She got taken into custody and arrested for public intoxication. My husband and I had to make a very difficult decision. Should we go rescue her and bail her out, or should we let her stay in the jailhouse and serve time? First of all, we considered the cost to bail her out of jail. Though not struggling financially, we did not have an excess of money at that time, either. We did not want to spend hundreds, if not thousands of our own hard-earned money to bail Kelli out of jail for an offense she willingly committed. We had some tough question to discuss such as, "What will people think of us if they find out that we had a daughter in jail?" Putting aside our pride deemed easier said than done. We thought of ourselves as good, upstanding, church-going citizens. Then we thought about if we decided not to bail her out, would people look down on us for leaving her in jail in shame? We remembered and discussed our belief in using "tough love" with Kelli. Tough love meant we should not rescue her from difficult situations and consequences that she created on her own. We loved Kelli very much and did not want to see her suffer. We struggled with our difficult dilemma of whether to bail her out of jail or not.

After Aaron and I prayed to the Lord for Godly wisdom, I spoke to Kelli and told her that we decided not to bail her out of jail. I told her that we loved her very much and that this was not an easy decision to make. I let her know that I felt so sorry that she had gotten into this mess and that it really hurt me to think about her spending time in jail, but we had to do what we thought best. I explained to my daughter that we believed that she most likely had committed the accused crime, and that she should serve her time in jail, which would most likely only be a few days. It hurt me to know that she felt betrayed by her stepfather and me, and it was not an easy decision. Through heartbreaking contemplation, Aaron and I came to the challenging conclusion not to bail our daughter out of jail, even though, I imagine some parents would disagree with that. We had decided to use the "tough love" method, and we agreed to stick to it, no matter what. We also felt it vital to set a precedent in the unfortunate, but realistic possibility of a future repeat of this incident. How many parents of renegade children bail their child out of trouble, only to have the child repeat the offense over and over again? It did not feel good to have Kelli think of my husband and me as "the bad guys", but even so, we refused to enable her to continue down the road to self-destruction.

Unfortunately, on another occasion, Kelli served a much longer jail sentence. This time for the offense of committing grand theft auto. She went to court and the judge convicted her of the crime even though Kelli had an elaborate story claiming her innocence. She contended that she got into a car in a Target parking lot with a group of friends not knowing that it was a stolen vehicle. One of her friends asked Kelli to drive them around that day, telling her they had "borrowed" the car from a friend, according to Kelli's story. She insisted that the others in the group "framed" her for the crime. Sadly, I could not trust Kelli's stories anymore due to her habit of lying to us many times previously. She served an eight-month jail sentence in the Galveston County jail in Galveston, Texas.

Even though I grieved for Kelli's unfortunate circumstance, the time she spent in the county jail actually brought me relief and comfort. It may seem strange for a mother to feel relieved about her daughter being in jail, but the stress caused from watching a child walk in their addictions, knowing that every day could potentially be their last day alive, is mentally exhausting. At least while they are in jail, they are away from the problems caused by drugs. Living with an addict, you never know what dangers they will get into while desperately seeking their next high. Questions pop into your head, such as, *What if she dies from a drug overdose? What will happen if she gets in a car accident while under the influence of a drug?* Or we think, *How tragic it will be if she causes the death of another individual while driving under the influence! I hope she does not get into a dangerous altercation while buying drugs.* Many times I wondered, *What if Melodi gets hurt while in Kelli's care due to her drug-induced negligence?* With an addicted loved one, we must fight the temptation to dwell on the list of dangerous and fatal possibilities daily.

Thankfully, I had a peace that passes all understanding throughout this time. The love and comfort I received from the Lord everyday overwhelmed me. Honestly, I even had astounding joy in that season of my life, joy that did not make sense due to my circumstance. The Lord healed me from depression by leading my husband and me to a new church where Pastors John and Mary Fowler prayed for me the first time I attended, and I never looked back after that.

God gave me the lifesaving message to stop blaming myself for Kelli's addiction, and to renounce the negative thoughts and words I spoke about myself. My Heavenly Father spoke to me through my pastor, Greg Thurstonson, enlightening me of His love, and blessing me beyond belief.

I did encounter a doubter from time to time. Every now and then a friend or acquaintance expressed their confusion in my faith and trust in the Lord and even frowned upon my joyful personality. *How could a mother with a drug addicted daughter serving time in the penitentiary act like everything is normal, and seem "happy-go-lucky" all the time?* I imagined some formed such opinions of me, or even worse. Not surprisingly, some judged me and questioned my sanity. During my journey, I had two people, on two separate occasions, specifically divulge their negative feelings about my mothering techniques. I was not doing enough to adequately help my daughter, in their opinions. One friend, whom I had looked to for moral support often, expressed how she would have done things differently if her child were walking the same path as Kelli. She told me, "If that were my daughter, I would do much more to protect her. I would chase her down and follow her everywhere. I would go to her drug dealer's house. I would go to her residence, drag her out, and take her to a drug rehabilitation center. I would not just sit idly by doing nothing and let her kill herself." Having a trusted friend deliver those judgmental words hurt deeply. I fought the temptation to doubt myself again. I almost forgot the directions the Lord gave me to not blame myself for Kelli's problems. I had to renounce my friend's thoughtless words, and not allow condemnation to come back into my mind over my life. I reminded myself that I did plenty to help my daughter. That woman was not walking in my shoes and had no right to criticize me or judge me. Experience had taught me that I should not shield my daughter from natural consequences she brought on herself. I used the "tough love" approach, which was not always an easy concept to embrace or follow. I prayed for Kelli constantly. I stepped in and guided her as the Lord gave me wisdom. I helped her whenever I could, and reminded her how much I loved her and wanted the best for her life. I had to completely trust my God to fight my battles, deliver my daughter from drug addiction, and heal her mentally and spiritually.

Thankfully, the Lord blessed my husband Aaron and me with Godly wisdom as we stayed faithful to Him. We continued to fight the uphill battles of dealing with Kelli and those who did not believe in our methods. We prayed for Kelli constantly, and included fasting with prayer at times. Our friends and family prayed with us and gave us moral support in our efforts to save Kelli from drug addiction. As part of the "tough love" approach, we made a rule to never give her cash when she asked for help. Believe me, she had many sad stories with elaborate requests that sounded very convincing as to why she needed money right away, but we stuck to our policy to never put cash in her hands. Sad to say, you may as well just go ahead and purchase drugs for your loved one with addictions if you furnish them with cash or give them access to your bank account. If I knew she had dire needs, I accompanied her to the store to pay for the items she needed. I wanted to keep the door open in our relationship, so I always tried to let her figure out life lessons for herself instead of lecturing her. Knowing the right balance to keep with your adult child remains a constant challenge. I did not want to seem judgmental, but at times, I tried to steer her away from inappropriate or devious practices. I reminded Kelli occasionally that we would be happy to help her find a good drug rehabilitation center any time she felt ready. I talked to her on this subject with gentle precaution, not wanting to poke the bear and make her mad, closing the door of communication.

Staying close to Kelli held many challenges due to her lying and attempts to take advantage of us frequently. At times we definitely felt jaded. We did our best to call her out on her dishonesties, even though, most of the time, she denied any wrongdoing. We had to stop letting her borrow things from us, especially our car, because of distrust. She fooled us regarding borrowing money too many times. She finally stopped asking to borrow money from us after several times that we denied her requests. We could not trust her to use the borrowed money for what she claimed she needed. When she found herself in physical danger, she knew she could call me at any hour of the day or night, and I would come help her. Other than that, we did not bail her out of her self-inflicted predicaments. We continued to use "tough love" with Kelli, as difficult as it became some- times. We did not want to enable her to continue in her addictions. We did not want any more pain or bitterness caused by her taking advantage of us. I fought hard to remain unjaded. I battled against resentment constantly. I prayed for Kelli and placed her in the Lord's hands daily. I did not want to close the door on our relationship or stop caring about her even though I felt rejected, used, and abused by her many times. I knew that if I cut her out of my life, her chances of surviving this lifestyle would become even smaller. To prevent myself from wanting to completely shut her out of my life, I decided to change my mindset of how I viewed Kelli while she lived as a drug addict. I did this by thinking of her, in that frame of mind and living that lifestyle, as "not the real Kelli". This drug-addicted individual was not the beautiful little girl that I raised. Her addictive lifestyle altered so many things about my daughter.

Years of drug use affected Kelli's health and even changed her physical appearance. She lost so much weight and stayed very thin. Her weight dropped extremely low during her worst times. At five feet tall, ideally, Kelli should weigh about 115 pounds under normal circumstances. While abusing drugs, she sunk down to about 90 pounds or less most of the time. Kelli's body became thin and frail, and her once beautiful, cheerful, glowing face now appeared gaunt and haunting. Her eyes became sunk in with dark circles under them. Disturbingly, sometimes when I saw Kelli out of the corner of my eye, her face resembled a skeleton in my peripheral vision, and her eyes appeared ghostly to me. Sometimes I wondered if I actually perceived her "spirit-person" when I saw those unpleasant visions of her. I do believe that addiction to drugs causes a spiritual death, in some ways. However, I never stopped thinking of my daughter as a beautiful young lady, despite what I saw on the outside.

Kelli's personality altered from her true self during her years of drug use, as well. It was so long since I had seen her true, bubbly, loving personality she always had as a child, up until she became a teenager. I heard the theory that while a person is on drugs, they stop maturing and remain the mental age that they were when they began using. This theory seemed correct in Kelli's case, because at age twenty-five, her mentality and actions resembled a young teenager in many ways. She became angered very easily when she did not get her way. She refused to take responsibility for any of her unscrupulous actions. She always blamed others for mistakes she made. She often became manipulative towards the people in her life. We could not trust her as far as we could throw her, to coin a phrase, as she lied constantly. She abandoned common sense, for the most part, and made very rash decisions. She was a poor judge of character and her choice of friends really stank.

Kelli's lack of common sense proved quite dangerous at times. One experience Kelli found herself in came close to causing her own death. Surprisingly, even though much of her account depicted her own immorality, Kelli told me all the shady details of the event, which she usually left out when recounting stories of her life. One day Kelli and a group of her friends decided to get some drugs to indulge in together. At first they could not find the "good stuff", but Kelli had an idea of where to find some, and directed the group to a dealer's house. They pronounced Kelli the hero as they made their way to the "crack house". When the drug deal fell through, the tables turned, and the group blamed Kelli for ruining their entertainment for the night. First, they called her a liar and beat her up. Next, according to Kelli, they put her in an old car, tied her up, and poured gasoline on her purse. Then, they lit the purse on fire, and placed it in the car at Kelli's feet. Her "friends" then left the scene, leaving Kelli there to burn to death in the car. Kelli said they insisted she deserved this punishment for involving them in a botched drug deal. The horrific story is almost unbelievable. God had His merciful hand of protection on her, I believe, or she would not be alive after that terrible episode.

I felt shock and despair after Kelli told me about that experience. I thanked God that she amazingly survived such a horrible attack. Kelli explained that she untied and untangled herself from the ropes and escaped from the fiery vehicle without much harm. My heart sank reflecting on the hate those people had for my daughter that caused them to callously plot her death over a failed drug deal. It hurt me that she called such people her friends. When I suggested that we report the horrific incident to the authorities, she refused to do so. Of course, she probably feared police arrest as well, due to her involvement with illegal substances, or due to arrest warrants she had. Unfortunately, Kelli had to live with injustice many times, due to her lifestyle choices.

There were many other times Kelli found herself in dangerous situations and absconded death. She often drove her car while under the influence of a mind-altering drug or alcohol. Other times she rode in the car as a passenger with a motorist under the influence. Dealing with people who bought and sold drugs brought many potential dangers and sticky situations. The drugs and/or the drug deals caused irrational actions. Dealers have been known to kill a person over a bad drug deal, which almost happened to Kelli.

Thank God for His mercy. The temptation to live in fear came to me at times. I tried not to think about Kelli dying or suffering a terrible injury resulting from a debauched drug deal or an overdose. I pushed the thoughts away and prayed for peace and faith. I could not allow fear and worry to take hold of me.

I had many questions and frustrations about Kelli's mental state. As a woman in her mid-twenties, her immature, hyperactive personality exasperated me, and I wondered when or if she would ever "grow up". She could not stay focused on one activity for more than a few minutes. Her expectations of how others treated her did not match her behavior and actions towards them. She acted as though her mistakes should be ignored or quickly forgiven, but anything done wrong against her made her hold a grudge she refused to drop. She acted as though the world revolved around her, and she desired to be the center of attention at all times.

I used to wonder if she had bi-polar disorder. Most days she seemed hyperactive, but sometimes her moods switched, and she showed signs of depression. At one point she asked me for help with her mental state, so I arranged an appointment for her to go see a psychiatrist. The doctor prescribed an anti-depressant medication right away. I felt excited and optimistic for Kelli to try this. I heard the theory that some individuals who have undiagnosed mental problems are just trying to self-medicate, which, unfortunately ends up resulting in addictions. Maybe the source of Kelli's problems stemmed from a chemical imbalance in her brain. Kelli never went to a therapist or tried taking prescribed anti-depressants before. I desperately hoped that taking medication would solve many of Kelli's problems. *Could it be as simple as that?* I wondered. I hoped this would lead to Kelli seeking further help and getting treated for any mental issues she had, such as bi-polar disorder. Perhaps, I thought, Kelli's life would improve simply by finding the correct diagnosis and taking medication.

Unfortunately, taking the anti-depressant did not lead to any onset of Kelli's recovery. I called her about a week after she started the prescription to see how she felt. She told me that she stopped taking the anti-depressant medication after about three or four days because it made her feel weird. She said it made her feel dizzy and unable to think clearly, and she did not want to take the medication anymore. I explained to her that most medications of this type take two or three weeks to take the proper effect, and that she should not give up so soon, but she had already made up her mind. I described to her how some people abuse drugs, or self-medicate, attempting to fix a known or unknown mental problem, and that taking the anti-depressant might help her to stay off the "bad" drugs. She reiterated that the anti-depressant gave her a strange feeling and that she did not see a need for it. She made up her mind and I knew I could not persuade her to continue taking the medication prescribed to her by the psychiatrist. I felt so disappointed in her decision and unwillingness to pursue this avenue of seeking mental help. My husband and I talked about the irony of Kelli saying the prescribed anti-depressant made her feel weird. She sure did not mind taking illegal drugs that came from who knew where, and, no doubt, made her feel "weird", but remained reluctant to try something studied by professionals, trial tested, and prescribed by a doctor. That just did not make sense, and we felt so frustrated!

Melodi, however, loved the hyperactive, childlike side of her mom. Kelli and Melodi constantly ran around, tickled each other, and played games such as hide and seek, and seemed like two children playing together. They laughed, screamed, and never stopped acting silly and hyper. It very quickly became exhausting to watch. I enjoyed seeing Melodi have fun, of course, but I knew the endless silly games and rough housing caused Melodi to see only one side of her mother. Kelli almost never wanted to keep Melodi for more than a day or two, so she made up excuses as to why Melodi needed to come back home to me, usually earlier than she had planned. Melodi always believed her mother's excuses for sending her back home sooner, or at least pretended to believe her mother, and stuck up for her whenever we questioned why her mother did not keep her word. For several years, Melodi viewed her mom as the "fun one" who let her do whatever she wanted. She saw it as unfair that she could not stay with her mom and tended to believe her mom's implications that I kept the two of them apart from each other. Coming back to our house meant doing chores, eating healthy food, going to school, and an early bedtime. She preferred having basically no rules while spending time with her crazy, fun mom. She could eat anything she wanted, run around outside and play with random kids, stay up all night, and watch whatever she fancied on television. *Mimi Juju*, as she called me, *makes life boring and no fun*, I imagine she thought most of the time.

Kelli had a bad habit of making irrational decisions.

She frequently made unrealistic promises to Melodi, and I usually got stuck cleaning up the mess. Once or twice a year she promised to get Melodi a puppy. Kelli and Melodi went to the local animal shelter, picked out a dog, and paid a small fee, or Kelli offered to take in a friend's dog who wanted to give it away. Sometimes Kelli picked up a stray dog. Attaining the dog never proved a challenge. The problem came from working out the many details of caring for and sheltering the dog, which Kelli never thoroughly thought through beforehand. Kelli rarely had stable living arrangements. She went back and forth from living with a friend and paying no rent, staying with a boyfriend, or sharing expenses with a roommate. Most of the time she picked out the new dog before getting an okay from the roommate or boyfriend. She would fail to check into whether or not she needed to pay a pet deposit to her apartment complex management. Also, Kelli rarely stayed anywhere for very long and then finding a new place to live often became problematic for her, especially when she attained her favorite breed of dog, a pit bull. For one reason or another, all the dogs that Melodi and Kelli procured on a whim, ended up back at the shelter because it did not work out to keep them or rehome them. Kelli eventually learned to stop asking me to take the dog in, as I denied every time she asked. I always warned her to think it through next time she wanted to make a rash purchase. Unfortunately, she not only did not stop the impulsive puppy buying, trying to impress Melodi, but she had the nerve to blame me, somehow, when it did not work out, and they had to relinquish their new dog, yet again. I could only hope and pray that time would tell Melodi, and also show her, that

Mimi Juju only wanted the best for them.

Kelli, as well as her friends, seemed to wander through life as "lost souls". Watching the struggles Kelli lived through, and loving her unconditionally, despite the negative light she often tried to put me in, took a mental toll on me. I remember one morning in the women's Sunday school class, at my former church, when I made a prayer request. I asked the ladies to pray for my daughter Kelli. Most of the ladies in my class knew Kelli very well, as she had grown up going to that church. The teacher asked if I had a specific prayer need for Kelli. Exhausted spiritually and nearly at a loss for words, I replied, "Kelli is just… lost. Honestly, she has lost her way, and she cannot find her way back." Unable to express it any other way and hearing my words spoken out loud, that Kelli was a lost, prodigal daughter, broke my heart. I wept as the women in the class prayed for my daughter and me, and I continued crying for the rest of the Sunday school class that day.

Despite Kelli's drug addictions, mental issues, and difficulties she gave me and the rest of our family, I never gave up hope on her. I struggled watching her self-destructive behaviors, the way she falsely portrayed herself to Melodi, and the unfair accusations she made about me and others in the family. I drew strength from the Lord and kept in mind that drugs changed a person. I constantly reminded myself that we were not seeing my daughter as her true self, but as a corrupt, altered version of her. I knew that I needed to remain a positive role model in Kelli's life, to retain any hope of rehabilitation for her, and that I had to keep the door of communication open between us. By God's grace and wisdom, I walked the fine line between displaying tough love and, despite her abuse, keeping our mother and daughter relationship alive.

I am forever thankful for God's wonderful mercy. I prayed continuously to the Lord to keep Kelli in His hands. I prayed for her salvation and deliverance. I laid Kelli at the feet of the Lord Jesus in my prayers, asked Him to protect her and take care of her, and believed His promises to do so. I believe His grace is always sufficient for me! Grace, I believe, is the Lord bestowing something upon you that you do not deserve. The Lord blessed me with peace while I walked through that huge valley in my life, one so enormous and challenging, that it felt like the "valley of the shadow of death". I experienced peace, a "peace that passed all understanding" and joy in my life that made no sense looking at our life circumstances. Amazingly, my husband and I even enjoyed a life of laughter and blessings most of the time. My daughter's drug addicted lifestyle, the heart-aches she caused for her daughter Melodi, the bad choices and death risks she took, would definitely justify a state of chaos for all who loved her – *but God...* The faithful ones, the "church folk", commonly use the phrase, "*but God...*" to explain what our God can do. Just those two words. Enough said. We go through this horrible event, or that tragedy, or this awful circumstance, and our faith leads us to say, "*but God...*"

"We have faith that God will make a way for us when there seems to be no way." Isaiah 43:16 (paraphrased). "Yea, though I walk through the valley of the shadow of death, I will fear no evil: for thou art with me; thy rod and thy staff they comfort me." Psalm 23:4 (NKJV).

— 6 —

It Takes a Village

KELLI sporadically asked to pick up Melodi every now and then. Sometimes she requested to see her every three or four weeks, and other times she went months without calling or asking if she could pick her up. Melodi got to where she rarely requested to visit her mom. The more often Melodi saw her mom, though, the more her mood changed. Melodi did not benefit from the sporadic, unreliable pop-ins from her mom, but on the contrary, her mental state suffered because of them. Many times, Melodi displayed moodiness, including anger and sadness after staying with her mom. I am sure Melodi felt instable and never quite sure of what to expect from her mother. Kelli moved around so much, so Melodi had to adjust to a new environment and often a different set of people when spending time with her. Kelli tended to create so much drama in her own life, so unfortunately, anyone around her usually became drawn into the drama in one way or another. The drama going on in her mama's life inevitably transferred to her daughter, and she felt the stress and

— 94 —

tension as a result.

Melodi seemed happier and better adjusted when her mother stayed away for longer intervals. We provided her with a loving home including structure and routine, where Melodi thrived. Melodi's life seemed to turn upside down when her mama showed up to the scene. Even though Melodi had struggled through a great deal of sorrow already at her age, she seemed to be a fighter, and had grown a great deal mentally. She saw that not all kids lived with their mother and father, and they survived. Melodi now accepted, even seemed to embrace, our unique family unit consisting of herself, Uncle Randy, Mimi Juju, Papa Aaron, and our sweet dog, Panda. Her acceptance of her position in our family helped us all to grow closer.

Our family had some adjustments to make the first time Kelli served several months in jail. Melodi reacted with devastation at first. She started adapting to the situation quickly, however, due to her mother's past jail terms. The separation from her mother actually seemed to help her deal with life better. Melodi loved her mother very much and always asked others to pray for her. She even felt confident enough to specifically share with her friends and teachers at church to pray for her mom to get off drugs and be released from jail. They had altar and prayer time in Melodi's Sunday school class at our church, and she often went to the altar seeking prayer for herself and her mother. At times, she even opened up to her friends and teachers at school about her mom's incarceration. She had no shame or embarrassment in doing this. She remained brave and humble at the same time. I loved her maturity. Melodi's ability to share her feelings and willingness to reach out for help from others gave me confidence and hope for my granddaughter's continued well-being.

Melodi continued to mature and grow mentally while Kelli served time away in jail. The months apart from the chaotic lifestyle of her mom helped Melodi to deal with things in life better, it seemed. She did very well at school, socially and academically. She made many new friends and remained close to playmates she had from previous school years. One day she came home from school so excited. She told me that she met and befriended a very special little boy in her class named Link. She said that during playtime that day, she mentioned to Link that she had not seen her mother lately due to her serving time in jail. Melodi excitedly told us that after she told the boy about her mom's absence due to serving a jail sentence, he said, "What? Your mom is in jail? My mom is in jail, too!" And just like that, they became best friends. God always works in mysterious ways. The sad circumstance that made both children feel so set apart from everyone else gave the two a connection that no one else could understand. Now they finally had another who could understand the pain, suffering, and isolation that they felt from having an absent parent. Melodi and her new friend, Link, shared an instant bond, and I could see more healing occurring in her.

Melodi had previously bonded with her school counselor, Mrs. Tracy McCarley. At three years old, Melodi began attending the pre-school program at the school district where I worked. She had extremely wonderful and caring teachers Mrs. Charlene Courtney, Mrs. Sandra Willoughby, Mrs. Matejke, and Mrs. Matute. When they noticed Melodi struggling with feelings of sadness, they let her talk with the school counselor, Mrs. McCarley. The counselor and Melodi's teachers knew about the situation with her mother, about her addiction to drugs and about the times she served in jail. Each new school year, I requested to meet with Melodi's teachers so I could tell them about her mother, and how Melodi felt about it at the time. Her teachers and school counselors did so much to help her grow and thrive. Those wonderful educators helped provide a caring, supportive community for Melodi, and that meant everything to us.

Mrs. McCarley chose Melodi to be in the Pal and Pal-ee program at her school. This outstanding program allowed high school students to mentor younger, at-risk children in elementary school. The "at-risk" requirement ranged from coming from a broken family, having a parent who passed away, experiencing some type of abuse or neglect, having a parent incarcerated, or having a parent away in the military. The Pal and Pal-ee program hoped to help students deal with different types of grief and loss as well as helping prevent students from failing or performing poorly in school or dropping out before graduation. It also tried to prevent children from getting involved in different types of unhealthy lifestyles in the future, such as drug use, gang involvement, or criminal activity by giving them positive role models who spend some time with the child each week. The Pal gets the Pal-ee out of class and talks with the child while playing a game or doing a fun activity with them. Melodi loved being picked for the Pal and Pal-ee program and grew very close to each young lady that Mrs. McCarley and other school counselors paired her with each school year.

Melodi enjoyed many close friendships growing up. She spent time with several little boys and girls at our church that became her close friends. She had several good buddies she kept through the years from school. She had a couple of older kids and teens from church that seemed like older siblings and acted as mentors to her, as well. My husband and I spent a lot of time serving as volunteers at our church, so the people there became like family to us, and to Melodi, too. I carefully watched the people whose company she chose. I did not want Melodi around any bad influences, if I could help it. For the most part, I could not prevent her from being around her mom and her mom's friends, so I did my best to make sure she had positive people around her the rest of the time. It made me happy and I felt very comfortable with the type of young people that drew Melodi's attention.

A precious little girl named Lyla became one of Melodi's best friends for many years. Lyla's parents and older brothers also became close friends with my husband and me, and our son, Randy. I will never forget the first time we met Lyla and her family one Sunday morning. My husband Aaron and I served on the praise team at our former church, where we met in League City, Texas. Our pastor and his wife had a niece and nephew-in-law moving down from Abilene, Texas, to help out with our church's praise team. They had several young children. We heard great stories about Kendall and Vivi and anticipated their arrival. Their family told us about Kendall's gifted musicianship and their talent as singers, and joked about them both having larger-than-life personalities. We could not wait to meet them and have them join our team.

Aaron and I had gotten set up on stage in the sanctuary early that Sunday morning, getting ready for praise team practice. As we tested our microphones and tuned the instruments for sound check, the Massey family came in for their first practice, about fifteen minutes late, with no shortage of clamor and ruckus. First, Vivi came in carrying a baby seat, containing a bright-eyed, dark-haired, chubby baby girl, apologizing and bursting with high-pitched giggles as she strode in. Vivi set her baby down on the front pew, leaving little Lyla in the infant carrier facing us on stage, then she joined me and the other praise team members up on the stage. I could not stop staring at the adorable little infant girl in the baby seat. Her extremely large brown eyes never seemed to close as she stared at all of us and never made a peep. Next, Vivi's husband Kendall walked into the sanctuary in a calm, gentle manner, with a cool, collected smile on his face, carrying his guitar as he joined our team for practice. Little did we know at that first meeting how greatly this family would touch our lives, minister to us, and bless us as dear friends.

Aaron and I grew very close to Kendall and Vivi over the next few years, and Melodi became best friends with little Lyla. Our son Randy enjoyed spending time with the Masseys' three sons, especially, their oldest son, Noah, who became one of Randy's best friends. Other than singing and playing praise and worship music together on the praise team at our church, Aaron, Kendall, Vivi and I also got together frequently and played worship sets for our friends and other church groups. The Masseys came over to our house frequently. We practiced for gigs or just played music together for fun and enjoyed conversation while the kids played together. Randy and their boys loved playing video games in his room, while Lyla and Melodi played for hours together in Melodi's bedroom.

Kendall and Vivi transitioned to Dominion Church with their kids shortly before we did. When we started attending there, it felt great to be back with our dear friends and have Melodi and Randy back with their best friends. The leadership at Dominion quickly recognized the musical talent and anointing of Kendall and Vivi. Their charisma and godliness made it an easy transition for them to move into areas of leadership at that church swiftly. After Kendall moved into a leadership role, he had nothing but good things to say about Aaron and me while in meetings with the pastors at Dominion Church. Not long after, our pastor Greg Thurstonson also asked Aaron and me to join their praise team. Again, Aaron and I continued in our passion of serving the Lord in the music ministry together, and we greatly appreciated our friend Kendall's acclamation. I am so thankful for our sweet friends, Kendall and Vivi.

Melodi and Lyla became friends right away as little toddlers. They had so much fun acting crazy together and knew each other so well. Melodi said she loved being around Lyla because no matter how old they got, even into their pre-teen years, they still acted like silly little girls and could play anything together. They played games, sang funny songs, made up zany skits, and shared many laughs together.

Melodi had another longtime friend she met as a toddler named Elizabeth. Melodi and Elizabeth met in the nursery and Sunday school at our old church. Elizabeth's mom,

Michelle McHazlett, and I became very dear friends. Michelle and I shared a love for music and often got together socially to sing gospel music and play our guitars. We loved practicing the guitar, and every now and then, we performed at a coffee shop or for a group of friends. Michelle and I sang on the church praise and worship team together, as well. Aaron and I enjoyed social gatherings with Michelle and her husband John often. Melodi adored her friend Elizabeth and loved when our families hung out together at their house or ours. They had many playdates and sleepovers and were guests to every birthday party that each one had. The McHazletts even invited Melodi to come with Elizabeth on several of their camping trips in their recreational vehicle. Melodi had thrilling times as their guest going "glamping" with them, as Elizabeth's mom called it, meaning glamorous camping. No roughing it in the deep woods for them, but rather, nice resorts with clean amenities and amusing, outdoor family activities. Elizabeth and Melodi shared many fun-filled times growing up together.

Melodi met another one of her good friends very unexpectantly. After our family had attended Dominion Church for about a year and a half, the pastor asked me to join the praise team choir. The choir consisted of about twelve other men and women, including vocalists and band members. At the time I started, the praise team had a set of dress code rules to help the team maintain a consistent, classy look. On Sunday mornings, the praise team members wore black, gray, or white slacks or a skirt, and dress shoes or high heels. Our leader, Deena Thurstonson, and other ladies on the team assigned a certain color each week. Each member of the team wore a dress shirt or blouse in any shade of the weekly chosen color, so that our outfits blended together nicely. We enjoyed it and our team always looked wonderful. A very good friend of mine and fellow church member, Janis Garret, asked if I would like some of her gently used attire that she did not need any more, so I could have more outfits to choose from for the praise team.

I happily accepted this offer from my friend Janis, and we arranged a time to meet at her house so I could retrieve the clothing. Melodi and I drove to Janis's house one afternoon after school. After a long day of teaching, I felt exhausted, and honestly just hoped to get the boxes of clothes from my friend quickly and be on my way. Janis invited Melodi and me into her home so I could try on the clothes, so, of course, I accepted her kind offer. She introduced Melodi to her grandson Jax, who immediately asked Melodi to come out to his grandma's backyard and jump on the trampoline with him. Melodi and Jax played together for about a half hour while I tried on the clothes. After choosing some of the clothes and thanking my friend for her extreme generosity, Melodi and I left.

Melodi expressed her exuberant happiness in the car on the ride home. She could not believe what a great time she had with her new acquaintance, Jax. She said she had never felt so comfortable with a person she had just met. Melodi realized that Jax attended our school, one grade above her, and he came to our church most Sundays with Grandma Janis. We talked about how she had seen him before several times, but they had never spoken to each other or played together. After she met him that day, they started hanging out in my classroom after school and playing together, and sitting together in church. They became best friends. Janis and I arranged many play dates for them. Melodi said they always had so much fun together. Their friendship lasted many years.

Melodi and I spent a great deal of time at our church, not only attending services, but also going to praise team practices twice a week as well. As I practiced for a couple of hours each Friday night, our church provided childcare for the praise team members with children during this time. Melodi formed many close relationships with several of my fellow praise team members' children as well as some of the children of the teachers and helpers at our church. She had two little girls that she especially enjoyed spending time with at church named Amaya and Sophia. She also loved hanging out with another boy from our church named Peyton.

Melodi also delighted in playing with her friends at her school in Santa Fe, Texas, where I taught. At the end of her school day she came to my classroom while I finished working on my tasks. Most days I stayed an hour or two after school, getting work done or preparing for teaching the next day. Melodi became buddies with several of the other teachers' kids in my school. I loved this perk of having Melodi befriend many of my coworkers' children. My teacher friends and I enjoyed watching them make up games together or play "school" in our classrooms. As a child, I always felt a little jealous of the teachers' kids at my school. It seemed like a lot of fun getting to play at the school after hours. Melodi and her friends sure seemed to enjoy it!

One of my good friends and coworkers, Pam Keller,

had two sons, Alex and Grant. Melodi met Alex at just three years old in a pre-school class in our school district. They remained friends all throughout their elementary years, playing in the playground, or having fun in one of our class-rooms at the end of the school day. They also had play dates and attended each other's birthday parties. Pam and I got together with several other of our coworkers and had "American Idol" parties. We loved talking about the con-testants of the singing talent show, American Idol, and at the end of the season, we joined with some of our other coworkers to view the season finale and watch the announcement of the season's winner. Melodi, along with many other teachers' kids, shared a special bond and had some great times playing together in the schoolhouse, or at the home of one of our teacher friends.

I am so thankful that Melodi had such a wonderful support system growing up. So many of the church leaders and volunteers helped Melodi throughout her childhood. She had a lot to deal with emotionally and became over-whelmed with her struggles and concerns about her mom at times. She loved her Friday night babysitter, Cory Garcia, who watched the kids at the church during our praise team practice. Cory attended a local high school and belonged to the youth group at our church, and he had a great rapport with the children. They played games and had a blast together, but more importantly, Cory helped Melodi when she felt sad. Melodi felt comfortable enough with him to talk about her life issues and the problems with her mom and how they affected her. He provided exactly what she needed, a listening ear, while she expressed her problems and sadness. He always prayed for her and her mom, and helped her cope with her struggles, giving her hope of better days to come. The Lord blessed Melodi with many precious people in her life, such as her favorite children's church leaders, Kacey and Aaron Martinez. They helped her grow tremendously, spiritually and mentally, and became invaluable to her as mentors and teachers. Other wonderful teachers from our church helped her as well, such as Melissa LeClare, Emily LeClare, Diane Sommerville, Kelle Blout, Bill and Becky Day, Laurie Tangadahl, Shannon Bailey, Johnathan and Sarah Randolph, and Lizz Brandt. It is important to get involved with and belong to a community, and our church family blessed Melodi greatly. I am so thankful for our "village".

Aaron and I had many great friends that we loved dearly throughout the years. Both Aaron and I share a passion for music, as do most of our friends. We spent many Saturday nights with a fantastic group of people eating, talking, laughing, and playing music together. For many wonderful years, our group we hung out with the most contained two married couples, Tom and Robin Holmes and Ben and Lizz Brandt, and one single man named Jeff Morton. We all met at our old church playing music and singing in the church worship band. Aaron and I, along with this group of friends, enjoyed the contemporary worship music of our church, but we truly felt passionate for Christian rock music. We decided to start a Christian youth rock band and called it The Edge Band. In the early days of getting together, we mostly hung out at Jeff's house playing extremely loud Christian rock music. Ben and Jeff played electric guitar very well. Tom and I played the acoustic guitar, Aaron played the bass guitar,

Robin played the piano, and Lizz sang. Most of us sang as well, so we took turns singing lead vocals, while the rest sang back-up parts in harmony.

Aaron and I had great times playing in The Edge Band with our friends. Most of the members of the band, including Aaron and I, had young children when we first started the band, so we brought them along to our practices and let them play together, while the littlest ones played in a playpen. The youngsters became best friends as well. Our lead guitar player, Jeff, remained a bachelor during that time, much to his dismay. He very much wanted a wife, so the other ladies and I often planned and schemed about ways of finding a woman worthy of dating our shy, bachelor friend. He did date a few of the young women that we set him up with and had one or two girlfriends over the years, but Jeff reached his upper forties and still had no wife. We wondered when or if marriage would ever happen for him, as his heart desired.

Our group, The Edge Band, played several gigs for youth groups at various churches and youth functions. We had great times at our practices and playing a few gigs now and then. We also practiced at Tom and Robin's house out in the country in Alvin, Texas. Of course, we always shared a meal before practice, and had plenty of laughs and coffee each time, as well. Even after our band stopped playing gigs, we continued to get together to share meals and play music at each other's homes for fun and fellowship. Happily, Jeff finally did meet a sweet lady and they began to date. Lizz introduced Jeff to her friend and hair dresser, Lourdes. They dated for about a year before deciding to get married. We had a wonderful celebration at Jeff and

Lourdes' wedding and reception. Jeff's wife loves Christian music and adores watching her husband, Jeff, play the electric guitar. After about two years of marriage, Lourdes had a sweet little baby boy named Ezra. We all felt pure joy that God gave Jeff the desire of his heart with a beautiful wife and little boy. Our whole group of friends from The Edge Band ended up joining Dominion Church shortly after Aaron and I transitioned there. Many of us serve on Dominion Church's praise team band together, too. Thankfully, we are all lifelong friends.

Friends and community are very important. We need to share life with others. We all have good and bad times, and it helps to express yourself to others. At times we need to lean on the shoulder of a friend and have a good to cry. Everyone, especially a person watching a loved one deal with addictions, can benefit from opening up to someone about what you are going through. Lay down your pride if necessary and take a chance. You are likely experiencing grief and pain if you have a friend, spouse, or family member actively living in drug addiction. You may have concentrated so much on the problems and pain of the addict that you neglected to recognize your own suffering. You do not have to hide the fact that your loved one is dealing with a drug addiction. The drug and opioid crisis in the United States has become an epidemic in our society. The problem is not the taboo subject that it used to be. Chances are, the person you decide to share with will have a loved one or family member, or at least know someone who struggles with this issue as well. You are definitely not alone. There are many others hurting and feeling a similar grief. Without exception, every time I opened up to a friend to share with them my feelings and inner turmoil about my daughter, a blessing of one kind or another always came back to me. We cannot give up! We need to draw strength from others in order to keep fighting. Set your expectations high to receive encouragement, education, and comfort. Once you realize that you do not have to suppress your feelings or hide your crisis, you will feel a great burden lifted off your shoulders and experience a new sense of freedom! The liberation comes by humbling yourself, becoming vulnerable at times, and allowing others to help you. Ironically, you will then see life more clearly and receive wisdom. As the Bible says in 2 Corinthians 12:9 (NIV), "[He] said to me, 'My grace is sufficient for you, for my power is made perfect in weakness.'" You can experience a new hope for recovery and healing, not only for the person you love struggling with addiction, but for yourself as well.

7

Trusting God When It Is Not Convenient

EARLIER in her life, back in 2006, Kelli had moved back in with Aaron and me, after escaping the abusive situation with her boyfriend Keith. She attended church with us and seemed to head in the right direction, back on track in her life. I had high hopes for her to turn over a new leaf and start fresh, and felt optimistic about her future of living a wholesome life. About two months later, however, she crushed my hopes when she revealed some shocking news. She confessed to me that before she left the abusive boyfriend, he had gotten her pregnant. I felt devastated. That seemed like the worst possible thing that could have happened at that time.

Kelli told me that after seeking the advice of some friends and family members, she had decided to get an abortion. I believe very strongly that life begins at conception, and always taught Kelli that abortion goes against God's will, but shamefully, when she told me what she planned to do, I did not say anything to try to persuade her against having an abortion. Instead, I told her that I understood that she had to do what she felt best for herself. I told Aaron about Kelli's pregnancy and that she planned to have an abortion. I confessed to him that I did not speak up or even attempt to discourage her from terminating the pregnancy. I justified my hypocritical actions by telling my husband, and trying to convince myself as well, that I did not want to be judgmental toward Kelli. Selfishly, I did not stand up for the unborn baby and its right to keep its life, but instead, I pretended that, as a supportive mother, I should not say anything about her decision. Instead of being brutally honest and admitting that I did not want her to have a baby because of the inconvenience it would cause, I reasoned, that due to the extenuating circumstances of her situation, aborting the baby made sense. Kelli used drugs. Kelli did not have a husband. The father of the baby, not a nice person, also used drugs, and had abused Kelli. He had dropped out of high school and had no future. Kelli had left Keith, or rather, escaped from him, and did not plan to reconcile back to him, despite the news of her pregnancy. I felt thankful that she had enough wisdom to not go back to him, at least.

Kelli had become pregnant only a few weeks prior. Yes, I thought, Kelli should definitely have an abortion. It made sense, and it seemed like a necessary and convenient decision. But despite all my justifications, the guilt of my hypocrisy started to creep into my head as I thought about her plans to abort my grandchild. I really did not want Kelli to have a baby at that time, especially having such a contemptible man as the father. One Sunday, shortly after

Kelli told me the news of her pregnancy and plans to seek an abortion, Kelli and I sat in church listening to the preacher's sermon. My mind wandered. I breathed and sighed heavily and my heart ached with turmoil. As I sat in the pew of the sanctuary, God's Holy Spirit spoke in my soul, and I heard a loving voice telling me that I needed to trust Him. He asked me if I truly believed in the truth of His Word, or did I only follow it during convenient times? I recalled my words and actions toward Kelli and felt convicted. I knew deep down that my reaction towards Kelli when she informed me that she wanted to get an abortion was immoral. Even though I did not come right out and tell Kelli to have an abortion, I did not suggest any other options or encourage her to do otherwise either. I thought about the fact that her innocent, unborn baby should not be punished or stripped of its right to have a life due to the mistakes of its mother and father and their ungodly lives. I knew deep down in my heart that this baby deserved a chance to live, regardless of the manner in which its parents chose to live. I knew that I could not control what Kelli decided to do, whether to have the abortion or to keep her baby, but the least thing I could do, as her mother, would be to offer her Godly advice. I firmly disagree with people having abortions, whether legal or not, and did not want my daughter to terminate her baby. Do not get me wrong, I also believe that if a woman does choose to have an abortion, she can ask for and receive forgiveness from God, who forgives all sin and brings healing restoration to anyone who repents. But I realized that morning, that if I had true faith in God and the belief that He never abandons us or stops caring for us, how could

I just keep quiet and not tell Kelli my true feelings, and not offer her the support she needed to let this baby live? I felt the testing of my faith so deeply at this time. I recognized that she may have been determined to abort her baby either way, but as her mother, and as a Christian, I should remind her of other options that meant letting her baby live.

Kelli sat in the church pew next to me that morning, gazing down and looking mournful. In the middle of the sermon, she excused herself to go to the ladies' room, walked away from the pew, and out of the sanctuary. I felt the unction of the Lord telling me to do the right thing and go talk to her that morning. I decided to trust Him and obey. I excused myself from the service, as well, and followed Kelli's path outside of the sanctuary. I waited outside, right around the corner, by the Sunday school building where Kelli had gone in to use the ladies' room. A couple of minutes later, Kelli came out and saw me standing there. She looked surprised, and said, "What are you doing out here, Mama?" I took a deep breath and said, "Hey, Kelli, I want to talk to you." She seemed confused and replied, "Okay." While the church service continued inside, I motioned for her to scoot over with me, away from the walkway, by a flowerbed on the side of the church building, so we could talk in private. I took a deep breath and said, "Kelli, I do not think you should have an abortion. I know it will be very hard, and I don't know exactly how it will work, but I know God will make a way. I will be here for you, and I will help you with the whole process, if you decide not to have the baby aborted."

Immediately after hearing my confession, Kelli's whole countenance changed. Her face lit up with pure joy.

She did a little leap and exclaimed, "Oh thank you, Mama! I am so glad you told me that! I did not want to have an abortion. I'm so happy right now." We embraced and Kelli's tension seemed to melt away. She told me that it deeply saddened her thinking about ending the baby's life through abortion, and that she dreaded the idea of having the procedure. She said she only planned to do it because she believed she had no other choice. She continued by explaining the great relief she felt from me telling her that she should not have an abortion and that she had my support. She confessed that it gave her the encouragement she needed to do what she felt deep down in her heart was best for herself and the baby.

I also felt so relieved after telling Kelli she did not need to abort her baby if she did not want to. I love that I obeyed the voice of the Lord and gave her encouragement to do the right thing. I knew Kelli's choice to stay pregnant and keep the baby would bring difficulties, but I trusted God to provide and make a way where there seemed to be no way. A woman should never feel pressured into terminating her pregnancy, especially if she does not want to. If a woman gets pregnant and does not want to keep her baby, there are options for her, other than abortion. One organization called Crisis Pregnancy Center offers help to women facing an accidental or unwanted pregnancy. Crisis Pregnancy Centers (CPCs) generally provide peer counseling related to abortion, pregnancy, and childbirth, and may also offer additional non-medical services such as financial assistance, child-rearing resources, and adoption referrals. (Wikipedia online)

Also, if a woman has chosen abortion, she needs to

know that there is forgiveness through Jesus Christ. She may feel heartache, grief, or guilt from losing her baby, even if she willingly terminated the pregnancy. God forgives and heals anyone who asks for this from Him. If heartache and sorrow become overwhelming, the need for counseling may develop as well. Many Christian organizations offer free counseling for anyone going through grief and/or depression.

I had high hopes that Kelli's pregnancy would give her the wake-up call she needed to turn her life around, commit herself back to Jesus, and get off the drugs. She moved out of our house again to live with a new boyfriend named Daniel. I saw some potential in Kelli and Daniel's relationship and wanted them to succeed. Daniel promised us that he did not do drugs and that he would make sure Kelli stayed sober and healthy. My husband and I both had a strange feeling about Daniel but could not figure out exactly what about him bothered us. He seemed so nice, had a wonderful personality, and treated Kelli wonderfully. On the flip side, however, he could not keep employment, and had a frail, skinny physique, usually bad signs. We wanted to believe good things about Kelli and Daniel, and had high hopes for their future. Daniel seemed to care a great deal for Kelli, and wanted to step in as the baby's father, but it turned out, they both lied about staying off drugs. They only told us what we wanted to hear to keep us from delving further into the truth. At that time, Aaron and I remained somewhat naïve about recognizing the signs of a person concealing their drug use. Our wishful thinking somewhat blinded us from seeing all the signs. It seemed inconceivable to us that any woman would continue using drugs while pregnant. I hoped the pregnancy would provide all the motivation she needed to stay clean. Kelli reassured me that she would stay off drugs, and I believed it, for the most part. Little did I know at the time that Kelli continued taking drugs during her entire pregnancy with Melodi. When she came to the end of her gestation, and the time came for her to deliver the baby at the hospital in Galveston, Texas, she tested positive for drug use, causing her doctor to report Kelli to Child Protective Services, or CPS.

I felt total shock at the news that Kelli remained on drugs during her entire pregnancy! I could not believe it. I did not want to believe it. I could not imagine any woman doing that to her herself and her baby, knowing the potential harm it caused. Miraculously, baby Melodi was born and had no physical or mental defects. Other than having a lower than normal birth weight, she seemed okay. She was healthy and very beautiful. Regardless of Kelli's issues, I felt pure love upon seeing my granddaughter for the first time, but also very surprised at her tininess! Due to the doctor's report to the CPS about Kelli's use of drugs during her pregnancy, CPS issued an order declaring that Kelli could not properly care for Melodi alone, and they authorized me to oversee Melodi's care. They allowed Kelli to keep custody of her baby, but only if I agreed to supervise at all times, so Kelli and baby Melodi moved back in with us. They made several home visits to check on Kelli and the baby. The CPS representative informed us they could remove the baby from Kelli's care and take her custody rights away if I did not remain present with them at all times. Kelli committed child endangerment when she chose to use drugs while pregnant.

At the age of thirty-eight, I had become a grandmother. It felt so amazing and surreal. I definitely felt too young to be a grandmother already. Anytime I introduced Melodi as my granddaughter, I jokingly told others that I expected nothing less than utter shock at my being her grandmother and not her mother. Despite the unfavorable circumstances of Kelli's unwanted pregnancy and her poor choice of using drugs while pregnant, I thanked God that Kelli decided to keep her baby and chose not to abort. One of my favorite sayings growing up, "two wrongs do not make a right," definitely applied to this circumstance. I just loved my beautiful, sweet new baby granddaughter. God had a plan and we had to trust in Him. His plan for us, I believe, from Isaiah 61:3 (KJV), explains that "[God will] appoint unto them that mourn in Zion, to give unto them beauty for ashes, the oil of joy for mourning, the garment of praise for the spirit of heaviness..." I especially like the part: He gives "beauty for ashes". I think of my granddaughter Melodi as a beautiful blessing from God.

Drug abusers often have very poor decision-making skills. Either they do not care to, or they cannot make wise life choices. Kelli continued down a destructive path after giving birth to Melodi. She moved back in with her boy-friend Daniel a few months later. That did not go well and led to me finding Melodi living in a neglectful state as I described in chapter one of this book. Soon after that, Kelli agreed to let me have physical custody of Melodi. After living through such a difficult ordeal of getting pregnant out of wedlock and then losing conservatorship of her child, I truly thought she had learned her lesson. But, unfortunately, she did not. Kelli moved on with her life, living on her own and back to her old ways, while Melodi lived with Aaron and me.

Kelli had no problem making friends or finding a new boyfriend. She met a new man and they starting dating. After only a few months into her relationship, Kelli found herself pregnant again with this fellow named Chris. Aaron and I barely even knew him. Kelli and Chris rarely came over to our house, and when they did, Chris stayed outside in his car and did not associate with us. We invited him in, but he chose to stay away. Aaron and I always wanted to meet Kelli's friends, and tried to show kindness to them, but Chris never gave us a chance to get to know him.

I felt completely flabbergasted that Kelli let herself get pregnant again. *How could she do this again?* I wondered. Aaron and I half-heartedly joked, "Had she not figured out what caused it, yet?" feeling utterly dumbfounded. My husband and I always used humor to get us through difficult situations, but this seemed unreal. We felt shocked and devastated… again! This convinced me that Kelli had not quit using drugs, nor had she made any progress in getting her life together, even though she tried to persuade me to believe otherwise. I did not see any signs to indicate that she had cleaned up her life this time. I had just assumed before, during Kelli's pregnancy with Melodi, that she would quit drugs. I thought motherly instincts would cause her to do everything she could to stay off drugs, for the sake of the baby to keep it healthy and allow it to grow and form properly. My assumption and wishful thinking did not happen. So, judging from past experience, I had no reason to believe in her sobering up during this pregnancy either.

At first, I felt complete shock, upon finding out that Kelli had become pregnant again, then I felt devastation. I did not feel joy at hearing the news, and it made me very sad that I did not get to experience the usual delight that mothers experience when hearing the news about a new grandchild coming. I had already been caring for Melodi, Kelli's first child, full time for three years. I felt exhausted from working full time as a public school teacher, as well as raising a toddler. A woman at almost any age feels a little run down at times from raising a toddler, but this forty-one-year-old grandma felt utter exhaustion from the task. *I cannot do this again*, I thought to myself.

"I cannot raise another grandchild," I confessed to Aaron. Hearing the news of Kelli's pregnancy made him livid. He knew how hard things were for me, raising a baby at my age and working a full-time job. We both knew, realistically, that if Kelli had another baby, the same scenario would most likely happen again, where I would end up raising the baby, instead of Kelli. She showed no signs of recovering from her addictions. My spirit felt weak at times, but my prayers for her healing continued.

I felt thankful and relieved that Kelli did not consider abortion for this pregnancy. Even a woman in the worst circumstance, such as one hopelessly addicted to drugs, I believe, should not get rid of her baby. Some may argue that it is wrong or cold-hearted to bring an unwanted child into this world, but I disagree, and do not see it as cruel. I believe everybody should have the right to be born and have a chance to live their life. A human may have a fabulous life, or a terrible one. The true test of trusting God and living in faith happens when we take the high road, even in difficult times or when the future looks bleak. We can trust God. Put your faith in Him and He will help you through every situation, no matter how challenging. Kelli planned to have an abortion when she became pregnant with Melodi, and I went along with the idea, at first. I almost allowed Kelli to go through with the procedure without offering her any advice or support because I felt the convenience of it would make things easier for all of us. I admit that I acted selfishly at that time. Thankfully, I allowed the conviction of the Holy Spirit to convince me to encourage my daughter not to abort, but to keep her baby. Even though Kelli did not change her ways and continued to use drugs, I hold firm to my belief that Melodi had the right to life. Even though I faced the enormous challenge of raising my granddaughter, I am thankful that Kelli chose life for Melodi. Admittedly, trusting God becomes very difficult at times. However, the ultimate reward most definitely pays off.

Please, God, I do not want to raise another baby! I cannot do it, Lord. I don't have the strength, physically or emotionally, to do this again, I cried out to God in prayer. *Please help us!* I thought about little Melodi as a baby in her crib in Kelli's dark, trash-filled apartment. I winced as I remembered the sound of her exhausted cry. As I recalled, it did not sound like a normal, *I need out of my crib, Mama,* kind of cry, but more like the painful whimpering coming from a baby who had sobbed for hours with no reply, almost ready to give up, kind of cry. The memory of that sound, baby Melodi's desperate plea, haunted my thoughts. I did not want this new baby to experience that same neglect. I did not want to raise another grandchild, and I knew if I did not take that responsibility, nobody else would. I knew that all the burden of caring for this newborn, in addition to raising Melodi, would fall on me.

Before I moved baby Melodi into my house to raise her, I remembered that I had sought advice from James, Kelli's biological father. He agreed that Melodi needed to receive better care and thought that I should take care of the baby, if possible. At that time, he claimed he would be available to help take care of her at any time, if I needed help. He encouraged me to step in and take over as Melodi's primary caregiver, and said, "Between the three of us, you, me, and your mother, we will all share the load of caring for baby Melodi, and it will not be a problem at all." That never happened. He never helped take care of Melodi, or offered to babysit her. He did not even come visit her. My mother did help me with Melodi a great deal. She loved Melodi and wanted to have her come over to her and my dad's house often. She called Melodi her "Pee Wee". My mom and dad had almost reached their eighties, however, and I knew they could not babysit a newborn, in addition to Melodi, that often. So the burden of this new baby that Kelli was expecting, in all reality, would very likely come back to me again.

I decided to have a talk with Kelli and ask her to consider adoption for her baby. I started off our conversation by telling her I hoped she did not plan to abort the baby. She agreed and said that she did not want to have an abortion, nor had any intentions of doing so this time. I thanked God and told her how proud that made me feel. As I continued talking with my daughter, I felt I needed to carefully present the idea of adoption to her. Kelli's drug use often clouded her judgment, I observed, and caused her to deny the direness of certain life circumstances, or to have unrealistic expectations about her abilities to handle them. She never came out and admitted that she used drugs to me. Occasionally, when confronted, she did not deny having drug addictions, but she never openly disclosed any details. She remained prideful and tried to come off as though she had her life together. This made me worry that she may, once again, plan to keep her baby, believing herself capable of raising it successfully. However, nothing had changed since she became pregnant with her first child, Melodi, so I knew it was unrealistic if she believed it would not be a problem raising this new baby.

"Kelli," I said, "I cannot raise another baby of yours. I love Melodi with all of my heart, but it is hard, and I am struggling! I am exhausted all the time." I paused to choose my words carefully. "I feel that you are just not in a good place in life to raise a baby at this time," I continued. "Do you think you might be okay with giving your baby up for adoption? We can find a Christian organization that works with you. I think they will pay you and cover all of your medical expenses." I did not know if I had all of the facts right, but I desperately hoped that Kelli would consider the idea. "Maybe they will even let you pick the couple that adopts your baby," I finished with my plea. We both sat there quietly for a few moments and Kelli looked thoughtful. Surprisingly, Kelli agreed to consider going that route, and said that she would think about it.

Kelli decided to research adoption and found an agency called New Life Adoptions. After calling the organization and talking to a representative, Kelli and I talked, and she told me that she loved what she heard from the representative about their agency. She planned to seriously consider putting her baby up for adoption through this agency. I felt overwhelmed with hope and joy. Kelli loved the idea of an open adoption and told me that New Life allows the expectant mother to pick the future parents of their child from a list which gives detailed descriptions about couples waiting to adopt. She continued by excitedly explaining how the agency allowed her to give her preferences on many of the characteristics of the perspective parents, such as their religion. Kelli had browsed through the files of some of the people hoping to become parents, and she had a favorite couple already in mind.

I felt so extremely proud of Kelli for making plans to give up her unborn baby for adoption. I also realized the extreme emotional challenge she faced. *Would she really be able to give up her baby?* I wondered. I felt amazed at Kelli's unselfishness. I marveled at how God could take what started out as a bad situation, and help Kelli turn it into one of the most generous, loving acts a woman could do for a couple. She could be the answer to the prayer of a husband and wife longing for a baby of their own. Kelli could help make the dream of having a baby for a barren couple come true. This unselfish act called for an incredible amount of courage and I had such respect for my daughter for considering this challenging decision.

Kelli giving up her baby for adoption did not seem like a negative event to me when I considered the alternatives. My mind went back to the time I found her baby daughter Melodi lying in the crib in mental and physical pain, in a trashed-out apartment, with all the adults there asleep in the middle of the day. I could not stand the thought of that scenario repeating itself with another sweet, innocent child. I knew deep down in my heart that if Kelli had this baby and kept it, I would end up raising it as well. I did not have the energy or desire to do that again. I had seen and heard of sweet little old grandmas that repeatedly raised one grandbaby after another for their wayward son or daughter, but I just could not do that. I felt as though I lived in a constant state of exhaustion already from raising my toddler granddaughter as a middle-aged woman. We still had our youngest son Randy, aged fourteen at the time, to raise also.

Kelli made all the arrangements for the upcoming adoption of her unborn baby with the help of the representative at the adoption center. All the plans sounded so great that it almost seemed too good to be true. The people in this wonderful organization, New Life Adoptions, treated Kelli so kindly and gave her great hope in her baby's future. Kelli felt so thrilled about all the details she learned regarding the couple planning to adopt her new baby. Kelli opted for an open adoption, so the agency shared the couple's names as well as many other particulars about their family. Kelli even got to meet the perspective adoptive parents, Duane and Kendra, during her pregnancy. She called me right after the meeting to give me an update. Kelli felt overjoyed after meeting them and instantly connected with the delightful couple. Kelli said that Kendra reminded her of me, her mom, making it easy and extra special for her to choose Kendra to raise her baby. What an honor for me to hear those words! Without giving out the exact address, they informed Kelli that they lived on a nice farmhouse in central Texas on a sizeable amount of land, and that Duane's parents lived on the property as well. Kelli learned that they had large family get-togethers often. Kelli loved this detail because we had a large extended family as well and enjoyed many family gatherings together throughout the years. Duane and Kendra had previously adopted a little boy named Reed through the agency who would become the new baby's big brother. The new baby would also have many cousins to play with in the family.

Kelli felt very excited about the choices she made for the upcoming adoption, but as her due date came closer, so did the mixed feelings, and she started having second thoughts about her decision. Kelli expressed feelings of guilt and nervousness about giving up her baby. I tried to encourage her by reminding her that Kendra and Duane seemed so awesome and could provide a great life for the new baby. I told her that she should not feel guilty for giving up her baby, but proud of herself for blessing a couple with one of the most precious gifts ever given. This couple had tried unsuccessfully to have a baby on their own, I continued, and they longed for and prayed for a baby to raise as their own for years, and she had the opportunity to be an answer their prayers. On a couple of occasions, Kelli confessed to me that she feared she might not be able to go through with the adoption, due to her guilt and anxiety. This made me extremely nervous! I prayed to the Lord, desperately, to help her do the right thing. However, I knew that just because I wanted Kelli to proceed with the adoption did not necessarily mean God had the same plan for her, so I prayed for the Father's will, and not my own, putting all of my trust in Him. Nevertheless, I hoped and prayed that I would not end up raising another baby, in addition to raising my other grandchild. Due to Kelli's life condition, I believed she should not raise a baby on her own. She had not changed. She had not received her deliverance and healing from drug addictions.

The caseworker for Kelli's adoption, Geraldine, contacted Kelli a couple of times each month, and as her due date became closer, they spoke weekly. Geraldine also called me from time to time to ask about Kelli's well-being and to keep me informed of the steps in the adoption process. During one of our phone conversations, she informed me about one of the adoption policies that made me become very concerned. She told me that after giving birth to her baby, we needed to wait forty-eight hours before Kelli could sign the adoption papers to finalize the adoption. I did not like that at all. I already feared that Kelli might change her mind about the adoption, and now knowing that she would spend two days with the newborn really made me nervous about the whole process. To be honest, I had hoped that immediately after Kelli delivered, someone would come in and take the baby away within a few hours. I felt that the quicker they took the baby away, the easier it would be for Kelli to accept the baby leaving. Hearing about the forty-eight-hour wait period made me so upset. I asked Geraldine if we had to abide by that rule. I tried to stay calm, but in my head, I screamed, *Why?* I told her that I did not believe it to be a good idea because Kelli might change her mind if she has to wait that long. She explained that the forty-eight-hour waiting time was a law in the state of Texas. Geraldine assured me that the law provided protection for everyone involved, and that we had to trust the Lord no matter what decision Kelli made. She calmly and sensibly reminded me that when working with New Life Adoptions, a Christian adoption center, we had no choice but to do the right thing. Even though it scared me, I knew I had no alternative but to accept her wise statements. I prayed a lot and asked the Lord to give me peace in this situation. Kelli had already made the right choice to let the baby live, thankfully, and I prayed that Kelli would have the incredible courage to follow through with her decision to allow this wonderful couple to adopt her baby.

A few weeks before her due date, Kelli went into the hospital in extreme pain. Her whole body ached, but especially her head. I went to the hospital to be with Kelli and to comfort her. When I asked her about her pain and what she thought may have caused it, she acted weird and seemed hesitant to talk about it. Kelli and the hospital staff acted mysteriously, and no one seemed willing to explain. Even though I still wondered what caused Kelli's bad headache, I stopped asking about it and tried to comfort my daughter during this time. The surreptitious reactions about Kelli's headache from the hospital staff and the lack of communication about it led me to assume that she must have been experiencing withdrawals from coming off of a drug binge. I suspect the nurses and hospital staff knew this but would not tell me in order to protect Kelli's privacy. I could not believe it. I felt so angry toward Kelli. I had convinced myself that Kelli had the wisdom to stay off drugs, at least during her pregnancy. She did not, and I felt positive at that time that she definitely needed to stick with the adoption plan. How could she care for a baby when she refused to take care of herself and the baby forming inside of her body? I hoped and prayed for a healthy delivery and no mental or physical problems for the baby.

I stopped asking about the cause of Kelli's pain because she made it obvious that she did not wish to discuss it. Kelli still had several more weeks until her due date, but while in the hospital that day, she started having contractions and went into labor. Again, no explanation from anyone, even though I asked. Looking back on the situation, I could only guess that due to Kelli using drugs while pregnant, the doctor decided to induce Kelli to start the labor process. I felt heartbroken when I figured out Kelli had continued using drugs while pregnant. As her mother, I felt dejected and confused that neither Kelli nor the hospital staff decided to clue me in about the circumstances. When her labor contractions started, Kelli called Geraldine from the adoption agency, who called Duane and Kendra, the perspective adoptive parents, to tell them that Kelli would deliver the baby soon. They drove to the hospital from central Texas and arrived in a few hours. Kelli had a nice large labor, delivery, and recovery room in the hospital where we all stayed in the room with Kelli. I got to meet Duane and Kendra during that time and they seemed like wonderful people, just as Kelli had described.

After a few hours of labor, Kelli gave birth to her second child, a healthy baby girl. As part of the adoption process, Geraldine from New Life Adoptions suggested that the adoptive parents cut the umbilical cord that connected the baby to the mother after giving birth. This special step helped bond Kelli and her baby to the new parents, and became a very special moment for Duane and

Kendra. I just loved how the agency thought everything through and made the process very loving and special for all involved. We all got to see the new baby and visit with her for a little while right after her birth. We congratulated Kelli for the great job she had done during the birthing procedure. What an absolutely beautiful girl she had! We all took turns holding the baby after the nurses cleaned her and checked her health and statistics.

Everyone held the sweet baby and passed her around as we engaged in small talk, but after a little while, the atmosphere in the room grew somewhat tense and awkward. Everyone acted very polite and spoke nothing but kind and sweet words, but I believe we all felt the elephant in the room. *What if Kelli decides not to go through with it?* I felt so nervous. She started acting sad and hesitant. She held her baby and cried. We did not know her thoughts or notions. I imagined how brutal it must have felt for her. It made me anxious to see Kelli holding the baby. I did not wish to hurt her, but I knew that she often made very immature and irrational decisions in life. I worried that she would bond with the baby, and then change her mind about the adoption. I had heard that in the old days, if a mother planned to give her baby up for adoption, they took it away as soon as she gave birth, and the mother did not even see it or get to hold it. As cruel as that sounds, it would seem to make it easier to give up the baby that way.

I did feel love for the precious baby girl instantly, but I strongly believed letting this couple adopt her gave the baby the best chance for a happy, safe, and blessed life. I felt confident in the agency's screening process of scrutinizing potential adoptive parents and researching them with background checks. I saw Duane and Kendra as a loving, Christian couple who could not conceive on their own, and seemed very genuine in their proclamation to raise Kelli's baby to the best of their ability in a nice home in the country. Duane made a good living, enabling Kendra to stay home and raise the children, which included Kelli's new baby and the little boy they previously adopted. I trusted God and felt a peace about the wonderful environment these two planned to provide while raising Kelli's new little baby.

In my opinion, forty-eight hours seemed too long of a wait time to make the adoption official. I did not want Kelli to change her mind and think that she should keep the baby. I knew that Kelli still lived a life of addiction and could not take care of a baby on her own. Giving birth to Melodi did not cause her to straighten out her life, so why should we believe this new baby would motivate her to clean up her act either? I felt certain that if she kept the baby, it would end up neglected, and I would end up raising another grandbaby. I cringed at this thought. I did not have the energy to care for another newborn baby full time. That may sound selfish to some, but on the contrary, I only had the baby's best interest at heart. I genuinely wanted the best for this precious new life.

Kelli stayed in the hospital for two more days with the baby. She cried almost the whole time. It worked out well that they had her stay in the hospital for that long because doctors usually have the mother and newborn go home after one day under normal conditions. I felt so relieved that they did not send her home with the baby during the forty-eight-hour wait time, as I worried that taking the baby home might encourage a stronger attachment, making it harder for her to proceed with the adoption. I was on pins and needles the whole forty-eight hour waiting period. Kelli's sorrow and tears concerned me terribly. What a painful and challenging time! I wanted to comfort her but did not wish to advance her remorsefulness to the point where she would change her mind. I kept reminding her of the beauty and unselfishness in her plan to follow through with the adoption procedure for Kendra. Duane and Kendra came to visit Kelli and the baby the day after her birth. I sensed their nervousness about Kelli's disposition as well.

Duane and Kendra showed such compassion and grace toward Kelli. They did not act forceful or impatient with her at all. They spoke kind words and expressed gratitude to Kelli for her future act of unselfishness in turning her baby over to them to raise as their own. Their peaceful, gentle nature and genuine sincerity blessed Kelli with exactly what she needed. They began to feel like part of the family to Kelli, and to me as well. God sure knew how to pick them! I stayed at the hospital for several hours the day after the birth of the baby to support and love on Kelli.

Before I arrived on the second day after the birth, Kelli called me from the hospital and told me that Geraldine from the adoption agency had come, along with Duane and Kendra, to finalize the adoption. I quickly drove to the hospital to give my support to Kelli and the adoptive parents. When I arrived, Kelli still sat in her bed in the birthing room holding the baby in her arms. She looked up at me with tears streaming down her face as I approached her and the baby. I put my hand on her shoulder and looked at her lovingly and soberly. Kelli told me in between sniffles that she had picked out the middle name for the baby. The agency allowed the birth mother to choose the legal middle name for their baby, and let the adoptive parents give the baby its first name. I embraced my daughter and my new grandbaby for several minutes while Kelli wept. Then she sat up, wiped her face, and gently handed her precious baby over to her new parents, Duane and Kendra. She walked over to the adoption papers and signed them without any words. Geraldine and I left the room so Kelli could be alone with Duane, Kendra, and their new baby for a few minutes. They all hugged and spoke briefly in whispers. Then Kelli silently slipped out and left the hospital alone.

I said goodbye to my granddaughter one last time and quietly thanked everybody involved. Kelli and the new parents named the beautiful baby girl Reese Harmoni.

8

Where, Oh Where, Could Rock Bottom Be?

AFTER Kelli gave up her baby Reese Harmoni through the adoption process, she grieved for a while. The finalization of the adoption went very well, and Kelli felt satisfied in choosing Duane and Kendra as Reese's parents. However, she still struggled with the fact that she turned her baby over to someone else and, understandably, felt a sense of loss. I sympathized with her turmoil, and I hoped that Kelli could work through her sadness. Whenever we spoke about it, I encouraged her to hold her head up. I told her that I felt so proud of her because she had done the most unselfish act possible in this life. She agreed, but none-the-less, her heart still ached from her loss. Thankfully, due to Kelli choosing an open adoption, we got to visit Kelli's baby, Reese Harmoni, and the adoptive parents, Duane and Kendra, once or twice every year. The New Life Adoptions agency held an event called the Kinship Picnic every summer for the families that met through the agency. It brought together all the families involved in the adoptions, including the families of the mothers who placed their baby for adoption as well as the adoptive parents' families. Through these yearly picnics, we also had the pleasure of meeting Reese's Aunt Audrey and her family. Audrey is the sister of Reese's biological father, Chris. Kelli never heard from Chris after she told him of her pregnancy. Aunt Audrey, however, became a good friend to Kelli and a positive influence in the lives of Duane, Kendra, and Reese Harmoni, as well as me. We also met Reed, the sweet little boy that Duane and Kendra adopted prior to Reese Harmoni.

Kelli still continued on the path of addiction, unfortunately. She cycled through friends, old friends and new, as well as a few different boyfriends over the next couple of years. Her life drifted along with its usual ups and downs, coming in and out of Melodi's life, and causing unsettling drama. We met Kelli's boyfriend Ben in 2012. He seemed very similar to Kelli's previous boyfriends, a Caucasian young man, with a slender stature, and a buzz haircut. When Kelli and Ben came by our house, Ben usually did not come in with her. Aaron and I did go out to the driveway to talk to him a few times, though. Most of Kelli's boyfriends seemed uncomfortable around us. Aaron and I always tried to act welcoming and unintimidating when Kelli brought friends over, but, for some reason, most of them preferred to hang in the shadows around us. I had a couple of theories about why they did that. Maybe their lifestyle gave them a feeling of inferiority around every-day, upstanding people. Or possibly, they felt guilt for not living a clean life, or perhaps drugs made them paranoid that people might find out about their wrong doings. I did not know for sure, but a majority of Kelli's friends seemed shy and unhappy. Or, as far as I could observe, they acted that way around us, anyway.

Kelli's boyfriend Ben usually stayed away from our family when Kelli came over to see us or to pick up Melodi. Aaron and I spoke to him a couple of times to try to get to know him. I asked him how he received his first and middle name, Benjamin Franklin, and told him I found it very interesting and amusing. He shared with us that his parents named him after his father. He said that he and his father shared a very close relationship. We also learned from our conversation that Ben spoke Spanish fluently as a second language. Aaron and I thought he seemed nice enough, but we felt that Kelli deserved someone better. Kelli already felt smitten with him, though. They stayed together and Kelli's life continued on the same destructive path with her new boyfriend, filled with plenty of drugs and drama once again.

Only a few months into her relationship with Ben, Kelli became pregnant again. When Kelli told me about her third pregnancy, I absolutely could not believe what I heard. It made me so mad and hurt! *How could she do this again?* I thought, *How could she let this happen?* She just refused to use common sense. Had the drugs clouded her judgement so badly, or, I could not help but wonder, did she have some other mental disabilities? I felt so frustrated and helpless! I wanted her to get her act together so badly. Why would a woman let herself become pregnant again after having not one, but two other babies that she could not care for properly? Why would she do this again after all the pain she experienced from giving her baby up for adoption, due to her inability to raise it herself? I cried and cried and wondered how we could survive this situation once more.

Kelli said that she really loved Ben, but she actually admitted this time that they could not care for this baby properly. She still suffered from drug addictions, and Ben did as well. Their relationship only lasted for a few more weeks after she found herself pregnant, as Ben decided to leave her. Kelli knew right away that she did not want to abort this baby. I thanked God again that she had the courage and love for human life to make this difficult decision. Kelli chose to give her third baby up for adoption, as she had done with her second baby.

Kelli contacted the New Life Adoptions agency again. New Life informed Kelli that Duane and Kendra, the same couple who had adopted her second child Reese Harmoni, wished to adopt another baby. We could not believe it. We felt overjoyed at the news. We wondered if this could actually work out because it seemed too good to be true. Kelli's first adoption went very smoothly, all things considered. Kelli loved Duane and Kendra and they kept in contact with each other throughout the whole process, even after they received their little gift from Kelli. Yes, Duane and Kendra became a perfect match for what Kelli sought in adoptive parents for her second baby, and now we prayed for things to work nicely for them to adopt Kelli's third baby.

Kelli had a pretty good pregnancy, and she delivered a healthy baby boy. Duane and Kendra came to the hospital when Kelli checked in for delivery. Once again, we had to follow the forty-eight-hour wait time after Kelli gave birth before she could sign the papers to make the adoption official. I hoped and prayed it would be easier for Kelli this time, as I agonized over that long forty-eight-hour wait during her first adoption. Until she signed the papers, I kept worrying that she might change her mind. Giving up Reese Harmoni had caused her some mental anguish after the adoption, but it had been for the best, and I did not want any guilt or sorrow to make her question her decision again and rethink the plan. Her lifestyle had still not changed any. She continued living with drug addictions, and the baby's father did as well. I knew she could not give this baby the proper care he needed and deserved.

The baby's father, Ben, did not have much to say to us about the idea of giving up his baby. He stayed out of the picture mostly. According to Kelli, though, he did not like the idea, which caused Kelli to question her decision several times before the baby came. Kelli's dilemma created a lot of stress for me, and each time she hinted of wanting to back out of the adoption, I talked with her and tried to coach her into sticking with the adoption plan. Neither Kelli nor Ben made any effort to give up drugs for this baby. Kelli had promised to stop using after giving birth to her first child Melodi, but she did not. Thankfully, I intervened and rescued Melodi from the crack house she lived in with her mom. Nor did Kelli quit using drugs after having Reese, her second baby. Once again, I had no reason to believe she would give up drugs to care for her third baby properly. This time around, she did not even offer a claim that she would abstain from drug use.

Kelli delivered a healthy baby boy. Duane and Kendra stayed by her side for the forty-eight-hour waiting period.

Kelli signed the adoption papers once again, after the allotted wait time. The adoption process did not seem easier for Kelli this time, as I had hoped, even though she had done it once before. She cried and grieved through every step. Of course, I did not judge her for that, as I could not begin to imagine the anguish she felt from giving up another child. I tried to do my best to comfort her and express my enormous admiration towards her for this act of unselfishness. I had so much respect and pride in my daughter for her act of amazing love and courage in giving up her baby to someone to provide her child with a better life. They named the baby boy, my first grandson, Raylan James. His adoptive parents, Duane and Kendra, picked his first name, and Kelli chose his middle name after her father. They took the sweet little baby boy home to join his new family, big brother Reed and his biological half-sister, big sister Reese. God works things out in amazing ways!

A year later, New Life Adoptions scheduled a meeting for us to get together and visit with Duane and Kendra and the biological families of all three of their kids Reed, Reese, and Raylan. Their middle child, Reese, had turned three years old. Her biological Aunt Audrey planned to come, along with her two children. I made arrangements to come and bring Melodi to meet her two half siblings. Kelli said she intended on coming, along with Ben, baby Raylan's biological father. I told Kelli that she and Ben could ride to the reunion with Aaron and me if she wanted to save herself or Ben from making the hour-and-a-half drive out to the center. She declined the offer and told me that she and Ben would meet me, Melodi, and Aaron there. Kelli said she really looked forward to seeing Ben meet his son Raylan.

Kelli called me on my cellphone on my way to the meeting sounding a little upset. She said that she and Ben had gotten off to a late start, but not to worry, they still planned on coming. I never knew what to expect from her. I wondered if she planned to back out of the reunion meeting and give us the brush-off as she often did. Her voice sounded strange when we spoke on the phone and I felt a little suspicious. She sounded high on drugs, possibly, but I tried to dismiss that thought out of my head. Even though she sounded "out of it" at times when we spoke on the phone or in person, I often denied the truth to myself due to wishful thinking. I felt emotionally distant from my daughter due to her drug-induced condition most of the time, and I hated that she did not seem to feel comfortable around me either. Maybe she felt ashamed or deceitful. My feeling of disconnect toward my daughter gave me remorse as well. I longed for us to be close as mother and daughter. I wanted her to open up to me and allow me to help her.

An hour and a half later, I made it to the New Life Adoptions center for our family gathering. Kelli called me again as I pulled into the parking lot of the facility. She sounded really bad this time, slurring her words as she spoke. I could not pretend to deny her intoxicated state this time. Through her garbled speech, she told me that she and Ben would not make it to the meeting at all that day. She explained that Ben did not feel ready to meet his biological son. He did not want to meet the child because he feared it would cause him too much pain. I felt so disappointed in Ben. I knew how much Kelli wanted Ben to meet their little boy. I hoped this letdown would not devastate Kelli and cause an exacerbated downward spin of drug use. It meant so much to her for Ben to meet Raylan. Kelli still struggled to recover emotionally from giving up this baby. I am sure she hoped for some mental recuperation by involving Ben in the process and having him meet little Raylan.

Once again, I found myself in an awkward situation due to Kelli's drug use. I felt nervous and hesitant about spending time with this group of people I barely knew without Kelli there. If you have a child or loved one with an addiction problem, I am sure you understand feeling like you have had your heart stomped on after getting your hopes up about some type of healing or recovery for them. When you love someone, you deeply desire to see them succeed, and you try to hold onto your faith in their character, but all too often the addiction pulls them away from doing the right thing. It can be so tempting to give up on them in an attempt to avoid the pain of rejection and disappointment when they break their promises to you over and over. God, help us to not give up on them!

After I took a deep breath of determination, Melodi and I proceeded into the building to meet with the families. I anticipated the visit to last for at least two hours, due to the distance we all drove to get there. Duane and Kendra drove about four hours from the Dallas/Fort Worth area, and Reese's Aunt Audrey drove quite a distance with her children as well. With the knowledge of Kelli and Ben not coming, I just wanted to get this meeting over with, and I hoped it would not last too long. I tried to put my selfishness aside for Melodi's sake, though, because I knew she really wanted to meet her half-brother and half-sister. I entered the meeting feeling very sheepish and embarrassed that Kelli and Ben had backed out of the arranged meeting.

I figured the agency planned this meeting predominantly for Kelli's benefit. As the biological mother of Reese and Raylan, Kelli had given up so much, and these meetings could help her to cope with her feelings of grief and loss. Of course, I could not control Kelli's decision not to come, but I still felt bad.

Once inside New Life's meeting room, we all greeted each other with introductions and friendly small talk. The atmosphere felt very welcoming and peaceful. I explained to the group that Kelli and Ben felt very nervous and decided not to join us, and I apologized to everyone on their behalf. They acted very understanding and put me at ease with non-judgmental reactions about their absence, thankfully. Kelli had called Geraldine, the adoption agency representative, before I arrived to inform her that they would not make it to the gathering.

Our time together went very well. Our group consisted of Geraldine, the coordinator, Melodi and me, Duane and Kendra, with their children Reed, Reese, and Raylan, as well as Aunt Audrey, and her husband and children. We met in a very large, brightly lit room, with three different seating areas, several couches, and comfortable chairs. The room had various baskets of toys, and the kids from each of our families instantly began playing together on the area rugs. We all spread out around the room in different clusters organically and spent quality time together, getting to know each other, talking, sharing stories about the kids, and having snacks and drinks that the center provided. Melodi spent time with her little half-sister and half-brother, as well as Reed, the older brother of Kelli's two adopted children. The kids rotated around the room and seemed to enjoy themselves playing on the floor together, getting snacks, or sitting on the couches next to Mimi Juju or mom or dad, listening in on conversations. Everyone referred to me as "Mimi Juju", and I loved it.

Kelli did gain courage enough to come to the next adoptive family gathering several months later. She felt very emotional and nervous, but she fought the temptation to back out of joining the group meeting at that time. She established a wonderful relationship with Duane and Kendra and her biological son and daughter. Reese's biological father Chris did not come to any of the reunions, unfortunately. Reese's Aunt Audrey, Chris's sister, continues to visit with Duane and Kendra and the kids on a regular basis with her husband and her two children. Audrey is a wonderful, smart woman with a big heart, and Kelli, Duane and Kendra, and the adopted kids are very blessed to have her in their lives.

We have continued to meet, varying the group, once or twice a year. Kendra usually plans the visits now without need of going through the adoption agency anymore. New Life Adoption Center helped in so many ways. It guided our families through the blessed arrangement of open adoption for Kelli and the wonderful couple, Duane and Kendra, not once, but twice. I thank God for New Life Adoptions and this union of families and the consequent reunions shared each year!

9

It Is Always Darkest Before Dawn

KELLI still trudged on for years living in the same self-destructive pattern of addiction. Nothing changed significantly in her life. Her existence resembled a roller coaster with twists and turns, and ups and downs, and more downs... lots of downs. I could not understand how she continued to endure a life of such turmoil and mayhem that she brought upon herself. Her stubbornness and strong will kept her surviving without seeking help. She claimed she did not need help. *Who would want to live like that?* my husband Aaron and I wondered. She kept cycling back and forth through friends and relationships. She went back and forth with some people, and others walked out of her life for good. Sad to say, many of them had poor characters and made bad choices in life, as she often did. She struggled to stay employed at any given job and never stayed in the same living situation for very long. She got into trouble with the law many times, landing in jail for several days, and on a couple of occasions even spent a few months in jail.

I never gave up hope for Kelli's healing and I never stopped praying for Kelli. I asked others to pray for her whenever the topic came up, or when the Lord led me to seek prayer. I regularly prayed to the Lord and asked Him to use Kelli's strong will for His glory. I knew that God created Kelli, her personality, and all of her characteristics. He made no mistakes when He made her, and everything about her had potential to bring God glory. I had confidence that through all of this, Kelli still loved God, our Father. I clung to a powerful scripture verse that gave me hope, Romans 8:28 (KJV), that said, "And we know that all things work together for good to them that love God, to them who are the called according to His purpose."

I will not lie, many, many times I felt tempted to cut off all communication with Kelli and shut her out of my life. She argued with me, lied to me, constantly made outlandish promises to Melodi that she did not keep, embarrassed me, and even cussed me out on more than one occasion. Many times, she had the audacity to blame me after she disappointed Melodi by breaking one of her pipedream promises. She twisted stories around, trying to make me the "bad guy", but, thankfully, I did not let her drag me down to her level. I let my good record speak for itself. God blessed me throughout the years with supernatural patience and faith. Otherwise, I could not have endured the mental abuse she heaped upon me. Aaron also gave me tremendous moral support, as did my church family.

At times, I considered that Kelli may have bipolar disorder. She acted rude and spiteful to me one day, and then turned around a few days later and acted sweet and completely normal, like her "old self". I found it odd that she almost never apologized for being rude to me or for cussing me out, but instead, she just acted like it never happened. I did not feel close to her nor did I trust her. I felt nervous around her most of the time because I did not know what side of her I would see on any given day. This caused more guilt. *Why would a mother not feel joy when spending time with her daughter?* I thought to myself. I felt sad that we did not have a healthy mother and daughter relationship. I had to learn to forgive Kelli and myself daily.

I know the difficulty of putting up with a loved one who treats their spouse or family member rudely, and I do not condone abuse of any kind. I did, however, choose to endure small portions of inappropriate behavior from Kelli sometimes, knowing I had God by my side and moral support from my husband. I wanted to keep pouring the love of God into my daughter and to be a living example of healthy spiritual and mental health, so I kept the lines of communication with her open despite her mistreatment of me. I completely understand the need to cut a loved one out of your life when they cross the line of mentally or physi- cally abusing you. During the many times Kelli had to relocate, and she asked to live with us, we limited her stay to a few days, or a week at the most because of that reason.

Kelli never abandoned her faith in God, thankfully, and she felt comfortable enough to join us for church every few months. Customarily, our pastor held an "altar call" at the end of almost every service. At each altar call, he invited members of the congregation to come forward to the front of the sanctuary if they desired to have someone pray for them. The message he spoke during each altar call varied based on the sermon preached that day, the general known needs of the congregation, or the leading of the Lord. Sometimes altar workers or the pastor prayed for people to receive salvation or healing. Other times the pastor encouraged church members to come to the altar with a specific prayer need, or to just worship the Lord while the music and singing continued. Kelli was not shy about going to the altar at the end of our church services, as she grew up in church and saw me and our friends do this many times. She sang or prayed out loud and lifted her hands in worship, along with many other congregates. This behavior did not embarrass or bother me at all, as I joined the worshippers in the altar on many occasions when not on stage singing with the praise team. However, at one partic- ular church service, Kelli's behavior during the altar call made me feel very cringy and uncomfortable.

At the end of church service one day, Kelli joined others to pray and worship in the altar as the worship music played. She had her hands raised and she started crying out loud. This was not unusual, as people cried in the altars at our church at times. The pastor encouraged the hurting and afflicted to come and receive prayer. Our spirit-filled church allows people the freedom to worship or pray in different ways, as they please. Some might pray silently, some might pray out loud or sing. Some people kneel at the altar, while others may stand. You could even see some dancing or jumping with joy, or at other times someone might be praying and crying. If a person stands or kneels in the altar crying and has nobody at their side, a fellow congregant or someone from the prayer team usually goes to that person to pray for them, lay hands on them, or talk with them, whichever seems best for that person's need.

However, Kelli's cry one morning in church did not sound normal. I had a strange feeling about the noise coming out of her as she stood in the altar that day. As I recall, it sounded similar to a normal cry, but also resembled a growl with a mixture of moaning. It made me feel a little leery and unsettled. Something did not sound right about the way she cried, and I did not know what to think. I definitely felt nervous, though. The service ended, and we all left together. On the way home, I asked Kelli if she felt okay, and she hesitantly said yes. This episode in the church altar repeated itself two or three more times over the next couple of months, and at each occasion, I felt very trepidatious about the sound of her cry. Some of my church friends congratulated me that Kelli had started coming to church and commented on seeing Kelli in the altar. They told me they were glad to see her in the altar, expressing comments like, "It is good to see Kelli getting so blessed by God," or "I believe your daughter is really getting touched by God's Holy Spirit. I have seen her worshipping and crying in the altar. I bet you're so happy!" I nodded politely and smiled, but inwardly did not share their joy about how Kelli acted in the church altar. Something did not sit well with me. I had a bad feeling about it. It bordered on sinister.

Then, on a Sunday morning church service in July of 2015, the truth came to the surface in horrible way. Church started as usual with praise and worship music and singing. Kelli and I, along with several other congregates of the church went up to sing and worship the Lord in the altar, as we often did during our church's Holy Spirit-filled services. After a couple of minutes into the worship service, Kelli started crying out very loudly. She also made other noises that did not sound holy, like angry growling. I did not like this and felt uncomfortable. I had a strong feeling that the noises transpiring from Kelli did not come from the Spirit of the Lord. A few of the ladies close to Kelli in the altar heard the strange noises too and began to lay hands on her and pray. I put my hand on her back and began praying for her as well. The music and singing continued in the service while we prayed for Kelli. She kept crying out, got even louder, and made more disturbing noises. She grunted and growled. Then she hunched over forward, put her head down and made some screaming noises. Needless to say, I became shocked and embarrassed, but mostly I felt worried and concerned about the welfare of my daughter. These strange outbursts confirmed my uneasiness about her actions in the church altar the prior weeks. I had started to suspect that Kelli had some kind of demonic spirit in her. A very disturbing realization, to say the least, but I felt grateful that I had several Christian sisters there praying for Kelli with me.

Thankfully, most of the congregation did not notice Kelli or hear the bizarre unholy noises coming out of her, due to the music's volume filling the sanctuary that morning. Then, the praise and worship service quieted down and started to come to an end, but Kelli continued crying and making strange sounds. Not wanting to cause a scene, the group of ladies praying with me took Kelli to the back, towards the door, and out of the sanctuary. We ushered Kelli down the hall and into the senior pastor's office. We closed the door, and my friends Shannon, Lizz, Penny, and I continued praying for Kelli. Two gentlemen came in the office with us as well, police officer and fellow church member Gabriel Gonzales, and the church's assistant pastor, Clint deGroot. I had never seen anything like this happen before in my life, except on television and in movies. I read about demons in the Bible and I believed in their existence, but this experience was new to me. Jesus and His disciples cast out many demons from people, but I never dreamed it could happen to someone I knew, let alone my own child. The transpiration that occurred felt surreal. It made sense though. My daughter spent years of her life putting drugs of all kinds into her body and had become dependent on them. The Bible refers to drug use as a type of witchcraft. Kelli had turned away from God for years and walked down some very dark paths.

I did not have a chance to think about all those issues in that moment of time, though. As we continued to pray for Kelli in the church office, she slumped down to the floor. The ladies and I bent down on our knees in the church office next to Kelli and kept on praying. We intended to rebuke the devil or the demon out of Kelli that day through the power and in the name of Jesus. Pastor Clint left the room for a few minutes, but officer Gabriel stayed in the room and stood by the door. He worked as a security officer at our church as well as attending the church. He stayed in there with us, I presume, to make sure nobody got hurt throughout the process of prayer and rebuking the devil. The church service continued in the sanctuary while the group and I prayed for Kelli in the pastor's office. We prayed loud and bold, proclaiming phrases such as, "I rebuke you, Satan, in the name of Jesus! I command you to leave Kelli and set her free. Father, heal Kelli and break the chains of the devil off of her, in the name of Jesus. I command the demon to come out of Kelli right now, in Jesus' name." Kelli lay on the floor crying, growling, and hollering miserably while we prayed. We beseeched the Lord relentlessly for about twenty minutes. During that whole time, we prayed boldly and persistently but did not see any change in Kelli's possessed behavior.

We had no intentions of giving up though. Those ladies and I knew by our faith and belief in the Word of God, that we had authority over the devil and his demons through the power of Jesus. We knew that God could set Kelli's soul free just as Jesus and His disciples had done for so many demon-possessed people in the Bible. However, after praying unceasingly for over twenty minutes, Kelli still showed no signs of recovering from her demonic fits. Shannon, Lizz, Penny, and I shouted out prayers and rebuked the devil in the name of our Savior, Jesus Christ. Finally, after about a half hour of laying hands on Kelli and praying for her, Pastor Clint deGroot came back into the church office. Pastor deGroot knelt by Kelli's feet, put his hand up in the air toward Kelli and called out with loud authority, "Stop!" At this proclamation, Kelli's cries and groans quieted down significantly to soft whimpers. The ladies and I continued praying for Kelli softly. Pastor Clint instructed the other ladies and me to pick Kelli up off the floor. The volume of Kelli's wailing started to pick back up again. The Godly pastor forcefully declared, "Stop!" again. He then announced, "Devil, I bind you in the name of Jesus. Let this girl go and I command that she is set free by the power and blood of Jesus. You have no place here, devil. Let her go, in Jesus' name!"

At that proclamation given by the man of God Clint deGroot, Kelli calmed down, opened her eyes, and began crying softly with a relieved expression on her face. I knew at that moment that God had intervened and set Kelli's spirit free. Kelli's whole countenance changed, and she had a sweet, humble look on her face. I could not believe what I just saw and experienced. Kelli and I embraced and the whole room breathed a sigh of relief as the atmosphere changed from tension to joy and celebration.

We talked briefly in amazement about what had just happened and hugged one another in relief. Then, we gave thanks to the Lord for delivering Kelli in such a powerful way. Pastor Clint told Kelli and me that he knew the pastors of a nearby Christian drug rehabilitation and said that he could get Kelli into the program right away. He informed us that the drug rehab center at Strong Tower Ministries consisted of a yearlong program for men and women struggling with addictions. He told us a little bit more about Strong Tower ministries. The men and women in the program live in the facility in separate dorms on opposite sides of the campus, with a church in the middle. It also housed a kitchen and work area, as well as a few acres of land where they held free picnics and carnivals as out-reaches for the community.

Kelli agreed that she needed drug rehabilitation and Pastor Clint arranged for her to enter Strong Tower that same day. Ms. Patricia Hendrick, a manager of Strong Tower ministries, planned to come to Kelli's apartment and pick her up that evening. It all began to fall into place so quickly! I felt surprised and overjoyed! God answered my prayer for Kelli to enroll in a Christian rehab facility. I praised God for taking such good care of His children and thanked Him for the faithfulness of His servants, Pastors Clint and Greg, and my prayer warrior friends at Dominion Church.

My pastors and friends became the hands and feet of Jesus and went above and beyond to help Kelli out. These people became like superheroes to me. My friends took time away from the church service that day, left the sanctuary, and prayed for deliverance for my daughter from the stronghold of the enemy. This challenging and exhausting task required great faith. Even though we read in the Bible about the many times Jesus and His disciples cast out demons from people, we do not see that very often in this day and age. At least, I have not seen it personally. I do suspect, however, that we probably need to see it more often than we realize. I still feel shocked that it happened to my daughter, but, honestly, not extremely surprised, due to all that she had gone through over the last ten years of her life. I believe the problems started early in her teen years with a spirit of rebellion. She rebelled against me and all other forms of authority in her life at an early age. She got into habits such as disobedience, lying, premarital sex, and drug use. Kelli received salvation and the infilling of the Holy Spirit as a young girl but turned away from the Lord in her pre-teenage years. She ran away from home and hid at a friend's house for a couple of days at only eleven years old. She also smoked marijuana for the first time at that age. Her rebellion continued and our mother-daughter relationship dwindled ever since then.

Pastor Clint did not stop at just arranging Kelli's enrollment into Strong Tower drug rehabilitation center that day. He also determined to stay by her side to make sure she did not back out of the arrangement. He arrived at Kelli's apartment later that day with our church youth pastor, Dylan Johnston, and Officer Gabriel Gonzales, the officer who watched over us as we prayed for Kelli at church that morning. Shannon Bailey, another friend who prayed for Kelli that morning, also came for moral support. I met all of them that afternoon at Kelli's apartment, as well. These people had become real-life *superheroes* in my book.

This group of angels helped Kelli and me tidy up her apartment and pack some things for her to take to Strong Tower ministries. Kelli thanked each one for coming and acted so appreciative for all their help and kindness. Her apartment looked almost as bad as the one she had a few years prior, with heaps of dirty clothes and piles of trash and clutter. We cleaned things up and bagged up a lot of trash. The atmosphere in Kelli's apartment felt light-hearted and joyous because of the amazing things God had done through us that morning, and Kelli seemed content, peaceful, and happy. We joked around as we worked together to get her ready for Ms. Patricia to pick her up and take her to the rehab facility. My spirit rose to cloud nine. From my experience with drug rehabs in the past, I knew they did not normally enroll a person on such short notice. I realized I had Pastor Clint and Dominion Church to thank for that. He had pulled some strings to get Kelli registered so quickly. Our church had hosted the pastor of Strong Tower Church as a guest preacher several times and our congregation supported the ministry in prayer, as well with monthly donations.

As the afternoon turned into evening at Kelli's apartment, something in Kelli's mood began to shift. She started to express signs of nervousness about going to the rehab ministry so soon. She made a few statements suggesting that she should probably wait for a few days before going in, so she could take care of some obligations first. Pastor Clint and I, and the others assured her that she should not put it off, but go to Strong Tower right away. Officer Gonzales watched Kelli very closely. He did not let her out of his sight. He reminded Kelli that if she had any drugs, she should turn them over to him right away. I began to feel nervous about Kelli's actions. She started behaving differently again. She did not seem happy-go-lucky anymore, as she had been all afternoon, but started showing signs of regret and hesitation. I hoped and prayed that she would not change her mind about going to the rehab facility. I knew she needed to strike while the iron was hot, and not put it off, or she might not go in at all. I suspected that if she dwelled on it too long, the addicted part of her brain might tell her she can manage her life fine without rehabilitation, or that she can just get help someday in the future. I did not want her to listen to that lie. She desperately needed a radical change that I knew a Christian rehab could give her.

Kelli continued to get ready to go to Strong Tower but did so reluctantly. She started moving slower and had a sour look on her face. Then she announced that she needed to pack some things from her restroom and excused herself. Officer Gabriel followed her through her bedroom and asked her to leave the door of the restroom open so he could stand by and watch. I silently thanked God for the courage and wisdom of Officer Gabriel. Kelli became upset and began to show aggression. She started yelling at Officer Gabriel and told him he did not need to be in her apartment. I became extremely nervous. I felt very worried now that Kelli would change her mind and refuse to go to the drug rehab. Nobody could force her to go. As an adult, she had to go in willingly, completely by her own decision. After hearing her scream at Officer Gabriel again, my head dropped in disappointment. I knew that she had changed her mind. The demon had returned. Figuratively or perhaps literally, evil had come back. Kelli continued yelling and banging things around in the restroom. Officer Gabriel did not back off.

Ms. Patricia from Strong Tower arrived at Kelli's apartment and joined us in the living room. She came to pick Kelli up and drive her to the ministry. We filled her in about what happened with Kelli throughout the day and how she started throwing a tantrum. I solemnly announced that I did not know if Kelli still planned on going to Strong Tower. Ms. Patricia assured me and the others that addicts often had second thoughts about their decision to enter a drug treatment facility and she had seen this many times before. Her words comforted me a little bit. Ms. Patricia went to Kelli's room to have a talk with her. She had never met Kelli. She began speaking to her so boldly. I felt so impressed and very thankful. She reassured Kelli that she needed help. Kelli remained in an agitated state and did not respond well to Ms. Patricia's appeal. She stated that she did not want help and wanted her to leave. She brazenly reiterated that she did not want to go with her to Strong Tower. Ms. Patricia stayed and spoke with her for a while longer, encouraging her and trying to convince her to join her at the ministry.

The air felt thick in the apartment outside of Kelli's room and I had a sick feeling in the pit of my stomach as I stood there quietly with my friends. We went from joyfully chitchatting and joking around as we tidied up and helped Kelli pack, to just standing still, dumbstruck and looking helplessly at one another. I frowned and bit my bottom lip as I looked at the door to the bedroom, and then back at my friends, our angels helping to save Kelli's life. The look in my eyes asked, *What do we do now?* as I looked to Pastor Clint for help. Kelli had now started yelling and cussing, declaring she did not want to go to Strong Tower anymore. She did not need to go, she screamed out, and demanded that everyone just leave her alone. My heart sank and devastation washed over me. Shannon and I went up to the closed bedroom door and tried to talk some sense back into Kelli. We spoke through the door, saying, "Kelli, you know this is for the best. Of course, it is not easy, but you are going to feel so much better once you go to Strong Tower." Shannon and I spontaneously took turns with words of encouragement, pleading, "You can do this Kelli. You are so strong. We know that God is with you and you are going to do so great once you get clean and sober. Your life will come together and you will have so much joy if you do this. We all believe in you and we are praying for you, Kelli."

Kelli remained quiet in her room. She did not respond. Ms. Patricia came out of the room, and we all just looked around at each other quietly for a few moments. Then I went into the bedroom to talk to Kelli. She did not yell, but she sternly told me that she did not want to go to Strong

Tower that night. She claimed that she planned to go the next day and now she wanted everyone to leave her alone. I came out of the room and sadly told the others what she said. "What can we do?" I asked. Ms. Patricia shook her head and stated that we could not force her to go to Strong Tower. Kelli had to make up her mind that she wanted to go, on her own free will. My friend Shannon and Officer Gabriel apologized and said they had to head on home. They each assured me, "We will keep praying for Kelli," and, "Don't give up hope, Julia." I thanked them and expressed my utmost gratefulness for all they had done to help Kelli and me that day. Ms. Patricia left as well after talking to Kelli one last time, with no luck convincing her to come to the rehab. As she left, she said she would return if and when Kelli changed her mind and decided to come to Strong Tower drug rehab with her.

Pastors Clint and Dylan stayed for a bit longer. Clint stood next to me and called out in a very loud voice, "I'm so sorry that Kelli changed her mind, Julia. That's a real shame! I know you must be heartbroken." I did indeed feel heartbroken. I felt completely devastated. Hearing the words of sympathy from my pastor caused all the emotions from deep within me to come tumbling out all at once and I began to cry. Why my pastor had spoken so loudly even though I stood right next to him, I did not understand in the moment, but it became very clear to me later. What a day that had been! I experienced almost every emotion possible in one day, it seemed. I was fearful and embarrassed when Kelli made those strange noises and growling sounds in the church altar that morning. I went from shock and bewilderment that morning as we prayed for Kelli and cast a demon out of her, to joyful delight and relief after she made the decision to commit to a yearlong Christian drug rehab. I experienced pure awe and sheer happiness from witnessing the unselfish acts of love from members of my church family. But then, sadly, the hopefulness and relief turned to nervousness and then sheer devastation as Kelli hatefully screamed out at us and rejected the help she had embraced only minutes earlier, refusing to go to Strong Tower rehab with Ms. Patricia.

My crying turned into weeping in the living room of Kelli's apartment that night, with the pastors still there standing by my side. I wondered what on earth happened. I had such great hope after what happened to her earlier that day. I saw a different side of my daughter after we prayed for her deliverance, something I had not seen in her in years. I missed that side of Kelli so much! I wanted my daughter back so badly. She seemed so humble and thankful for a few hours and expressed the feeling of freedom in her spirit. She said she knew that Strong Tower would be a place to receive healing. She acted excited about going there. Why did she change her mind so abruptly? Pastor Clint offered a hug to console me as I wept and sobbed. He loudly and boisterously called out again, "Julia, I am so sorry that Kelli changed her mind about going into Strong Tower. I know you have been praying for her as a loving, heart-broken mama for an extremely long time." I continued weeping out loud in utter despair.

Looking back on that night, I appreciate the Godly wisdom in my pastor, proclaiming his sorrow and regret, causing my tears to flow. God knew that Kelli needed to hear my mourning. She needed to sense the agony in my heart and the pain of my soul. I had not cried openly in front of Kelli in years due to unintentional numbness of my feelings. I realize that I had become jaded and had hardened my heart toward her after all the pain and grief she caused me. Although she lied to me, cussed me out, and made false accusations against me, I could never stop loving her no matter what. I did not tell her about all the sleepless nights I endured, crying and praying for her healing, since she had gone down the road of drug addiction. Sheer anguish and despair came over me as I wept that day, standing in her apartment. I strongly believe Kelli needed to hear my weeping that night, and that when she sensed my deep pain, it opened a door to remind her of her mother's deep love for her. I spent years praying for Kelli's healing, and now it seemed my hopes and dreams for her freedom from drug addiction might disappear in that moment. I did not hold back my sorrow or the immense volume of my lamentation.

I left my heart on the floor as I cried for my daughter. About fifteen minutes later, the two pastors and I left Kelli's apartment while she remained in her bedroom behind the closed door. Pastor Clint called Ms. Patricia and told her not to come back that night. He explained that Kelli changed her mind and decided not to enter the program at Strong Tower ministries.

10

A Miraculous Turnaround Leads to... Prison?

THEN something miraculous happened! Shortly after I left Kelli's shabby little apartment, forlorn and in tears, she called me and told me she changed her mind again. Kelli informed me that she had just called Pastor Clint and told him that she would like to go to Strong Tower Ministries rehabilitation center after all. She said Pastor Clint had already called Ms. Patricia from Strong Tower to have her come back to League City to pick her up and take her to the facility. *What?* I had to pinch myself to make sure I heard her correctly. *Would it really happen this time?* My high hopes shot up into the night sky again. "Thank You, Lord!" I proclaimed. We got off the phone at around 9:00 at night.

My emotions had been on a roller coaster. The ups and downs I experienced that day seemed exhausting and scary. That morning, I felt so thrilled to have Kelli at church with me, but then terrified when she started acting possessed in the altar at the church service. I felt so amazed and thankful to have so many friends by my side praying for Kelli's deliverance. I became ecstatic when Kelli agreed to go to the Christian, live-in drug rehab center. My heart filled with joy when my friends came to Kelli's apartment with me to help her get ready to go to the rehab. Then the devastating shock came when she yelled at all of us, told us she would not go into the treatment center, and demanded that everyone leave her apartment. Now, as I heard the wonderful news that she changed her mind and wanted to go to Strong Tower for rehabilitation I felt nervous excitement. I also felt a little trepidation and prayed with all of my heart for her to go through with it this time.

I looked back at my day and could not believe all that we experienced in such a short amount of time. I wondered how on earth these events took place. It felt very surreal. I wondered in amazement, *Did all of that really happen? Did we actually deliver my daughter from a demon? Or the devil?* I completely trusted every word from the Good Book, the Holy Bible. I believed that Jesus and His disciples as well as others recorded in the Bible cast demons and devils out of people, but I marveled as I thought, *Who do I actually know that has had this happen to them?* It seemed crazy! The day felt so special and ordained by God as I pondered the events. My amazing friends stuck by Kelli and me the whole day. They believed with me that God could do a miracle and we fought together against the principalities of this world in the spirit realm, through the power of Jesus Christ our Savior. I had witnessed a miracle and seen true acts of unselfish heroism. I felt like I had angels and superheroes by my side that day.

It actually happened! Kelli stuck with her decision. Ms.

Patricia went back to Kelli's apartment that same night, picked her up, and took her to Strong Tower drug rehabilitation facility. I believe whole-heartedly one of the main reasons Kelli changed her mind and decided to go into the rehab was because she heard me crying and witnessed my heart breaking outside her bedroom door in her apartment. I have Pastor Clint deGroot to thank for that when he stood with me, recognized a mother's pain in seeing her daughter suffer, and announced my devastation loud enough for Kelli to hear through her bedroom door. So many angels and superheroes helped me that day, as well as the years prior. Oh, my goodness, what a relief! God answered my prayers. Never stop praying for your loved one. Never give up!

Kelli entered the year-long Christian drug rehabilitation facility, Strong Tower Ministries, in La Marque, Texas. I loved everything about the ministry of Strong Tower and the treatment program. For the first several weeks, they did not allow Kelli to have contact with me or anyone else outside of the program. Most treatment programs recommend this as a necessary start to recovery. Addicts need a fresh start and a chance to form new habits as they shed old ones. They may become tempted to slip back into their drug-using ways if they associate with their former "drug buddies", especially at the beginning of their recovery journey.

When we officially admitted her into Strong Tower, we wondered how we could afford a year-long stay in a drug rehab. We felt so desperate to get her into the rehab that we did not think about the cost at first. Every other facility she entered charged thousands of dollars. One of the rehabs

Kelli went to previously cost $14,000, and it only lasted for a month. Thankfully, our insurance covered most of the cost that time and my mother helped with the fees, as well. This time we did not check with the insurance about eligibility of treatment, and the amount of coverage allowed. With Kelli willing to go into the program, we wanted to strike while the iron was hot and not wait around to inquire with the insurance agents, which sometimes took days or weeks to get a response. We put our hope and trust in the Lord to take care of it once we got her enrolled.

To our happy surprise, Strong Tower did not require a fee for Kelli to live at the dorm of their facility and receive treatment in their program! We learned that the ministry operated through donations and fundraisers and did not ask the addict or their family for any fees. We rejoiced and said *Hallelujah* to the Lord. What a tremendous blessing and a burden lifted off our shoulders. This ministry helps so many hurting people who cannot afford expensive drug treatment facilities. God bless them!

After about two or three weeks in the program, Kelli called me to give me a report of her progress. She sounded so good on the phone. She told me about her day-to-day life there. She lived in a dormitory room next to Strong Tower Church. The program required the students to wake up early every day and follow a structured schedule. Kelli and the other students in the program received their meals in the cafeteria. They participated in several Bible classes and devotionals. The staff and counselors at Strong Tower required the students to work at different jobs such as housekeeping around the church or in the dormitories, preparing and cooking the meals, or maintaining the grounds surrounding the church and other buildings of the ministries. The students had a few short breaks throughout the day, but mostly stayed busy on a strict schedule, either working or participating in group Bible studies and counseling sessions. Kelli had accepted Jesus as her Savior at a young age, so she embraced her roots, and gladly participated in the Christian teachings. The men and the women in the program stayed in separate areas of the facility. They built the men's and women's dormitory rooms on opposite sides of the church's property. The program discouraged students from engaging in male/female relationships while in treatment, in order to help them to stay focused on their recovery.

I felt absolutely thrilled with everything about Strong Tower's drug rehabilitation center and Kelli's progress. She sounded wonderful when I spoke to her on the phone every two or three weeks, and she adapted to the strict routine very well, surprisingly. Kelli told me that she appreciated the treatment process so far and had learned so much from the program already. She had a hard time at first, adjusting to the daily routines, she admitted, but realized their effectiveness to her recovery. She, as many other addicts, did not live a very disciplined life during her years of drug use, and she understood that this new way of scheduled, structured living provided excellent training for a fruitful life ahead of her.

Then, after about four months of treatment in Strong Tower, Kelli's wonderful new healing journey took a sour detour. I got a phone call from Ms. Patricia, the woman from Strong Tower. Oh, the terrible shock I felt when I received her call one morning while on my conference period at work. Ms. Patricia greeted me, then got straight to the point with her bad news, "Julia, I am sorry to tell you this, but your daughter Kelli has decided to leave the ministry." *Oh no*, I thought. *This is awful news!* "Kelli just informed us," Ms. Patricia continued, "that she is leaving the program, and that she has a friend who will be picking her up later today. Kelli said that she has learned all she needs from us and that she is ready to go live her life."

Kelli's first few months in Strong Tower rehab seemed to go so well, why would she do this? I wondered. I told Ms. Patricia that this news came as a complete surprise to me and that Kelli did not give me any warning about wanting to do this. I told her I did not agree with her decision to leave at all. Ms. Patricia told me that they could not hold Kelli there against her will and she reminded me that individuals seeking help came to Strong Tower treatment center voluntarily. They recommended the students stay in the program for at least one year, but, as adults, they had the freedom to leave at any time. Ms. Patricia expressed her disappointment in Kelli's desire to leave, and said that she had tried to convince her to stay, with no luck. "I just wanted you to be aware of what Kelli planned to do," she continued regretfully. She let me know that Kelli could reenter the program, if she chose to, at any time. I thanked Ms. Patricia for all she had done. I told her that I sincerely hoped Kelli would change her mind and go back to them. We said goodbye and I hung up the phone. My heart sank! I knew my daughter was not ready for life outside of the rehab yet. I did not believe Kelli had learned enough to leave the program and live a successful, sober life. Kelli had not said anything to me about wanting to leave Strong

Tower. I worried that her rebelliousness had come back. I felt so sad and disappointed about her leaving after all that we had been through to get my daughter into the wonderful program.

Why, God? I prayed. I strongly disagreed with Kelli's decision to leave Strong Tower ministries! A few days later, I finally heard from Kelli. She claimed that she had received all of the training that she needed and thought herself ready to live a healthy life. Kelli used drugs consistently for over ten years, even progressing to the point of intravenously shooting herself up with heroin and meth. My daughter had struggled for so long mentally and physically, with voluminous trials and tribulations, most of which she brought on herself. I knew in my heart that Kelli needed at least the full year of drug recovery treatment, not just a few months. My heart felt crushed at her leaving Strong Tower, however, I did not feel total devastation, or spiral into a state of depression, thankfully. Somehow, I had an unexplainable peace about the situation. I believed deep down that God had something up His sleeve, that He was not finished with Kelli yet… and boy did He! Kelli did leave Strong Tower that day, but God still had His hand on that girl.

Kelli understandably did not feel thrilled with what happened shortly after she left Strong Tower, but our God remains faithful and just in all His ways. I had prayerfully placed her in the hands of God. He heard my prayers and had no plans of letting her go. Warning! Be careful what you pray for and be ready for whatever God plans to do when trusting Him to heal your son or daughter or loved one. You can do this when you let your strength come from the Lord.

Exactly one week after Kelli chose to leave Strong Tower, nine months before completing the program, she called to inform me that the police had arrested her and taken her into custody. Kelli had been charged with a felony drug crime, which meant, she would serve at least a year in prison. *Hmm... very interesting! One year.* She should have stayed in Strong Tower for a year but chose to rebel and leave. She explained what happened and said that she believed the local police department "set her up". Ironically, I believed her story this time. A random guy that Kelli had not seen in years showed up at her door, out of the blue, and sold her some "good drugs" at a very low price, she told me. Kelli left her trailer a few minutes after that, she continued, and then the police stopped her at the end of her street for no apparent reason. They searched her and found the drugs. Am I a bad mother, though, for smiling to myself as we spoke on the phone, and she explained how the police set her up in an illegal drug deal? I did feel a little guilty for that, but not too much. *Yes,* I contemplated, *maybe the police did arrange a phony drug deal to cause Kelli's arrest,* but I knew in my spirit who really caused it. I discerned the root cause, the One who actually "set her up", the Lord Jesus. I felt like doing a happy dance upon hearing this news from my daughter, as strange as that may sound.

God answered my prayer when I cried out to Him, placing Kelli into His hands, and asking Him to do "whatever it takes" to save, heal, and deliver my daughter. *If it takes sending my daughter to prison,* I said in my heart, *to save her from herself, then let it be,* I told the Lord. I can see how some might think it bizarre that I found joy in the news of my daughter's pending imprisonment, but the happiness came mostly from the relief I felt. If you have a loved one struggling with addictions, you may understand. Living in constant fear of what will happen to this person due to their addictions can become exhausting if you let it. The terrible situations they get into, the fear of an accidental overdose, and other possible catastrophes come to mind on a daily basis.

I trusted God, and it made me happy that when Kelli strayed from His plan by leaving Strong Tower treatment center too soon, He did what it took to get her attention. I felt that Kelli might even benefit from her prison sentence. First of all, I hoped it would teach her that when God has His hand on you to guide you, you better do the right thing, or He will "get you". I say this jokingly. He will "get you" in a good way, I believe. I trusted that what the Lord would do in Kelli's life would be for her benefit. The Bible says in Jeremiah 29:11 (AMP), "'For I know the plans and thoughts that I have for you' says the Lord, 'plans for peace and well-being and not for disaster, to give you a future and a hope.'" Secondly, I felt relieved due to the simple fact that she could not use drugs while in prison. I realized that sometimes prisoners do get drugs somehow, but I knew, at least, the likelihood of it happening now would be greatly reduced while in prison. In addition, life could remain smooth and calm for Melodi, if Kelli did not come and bring drama in her life, as she had done prior to entering the treatment program.

I prayed that serving time in prison would greatly benefit Kelli in her walk with God. In time, I saw that God answered that request mightily and victoriously! Praise to the Lord, I began to see a huge change in Kelli's personality over the next few months. Yes, while she worked the program in Strong Tower, I saw great progress, but now I saw a new humbleness in Kelli. While serving time in prison, Kelli and I talked on the phone and through letters, and the complete joy in her character amazed me. I felt so pleased and hopeful about her transformation. She told me that the Lord spoke to her heart while in prison and gave her dreams. Prison was not easy by any means, she admitted, but she said she now felt closer to God than she ever had before. She explained that serving time humbled her and gave her a new outlook on life and family, and drew her closer to God in a way she never thought possible. She told me that she planned to re-enter Strong Tower drug treatment ministry when she finished her prison sentence. That news brought sheer joy and delight to my soul. I had faith that she would follow through with her promise.

Kelli served a yearlong prison sentence. She wrote us long letters every month, and Melodi and I visited her in prison every few months. Melodi and I traveled for two hours to get to the prison to visit with her. I felt nervous, especially the first time we visited. I did not know what to expect and felt a little fearful of the unknown. We drove onto the prison property in the Plains Region of Texas down a long road passing a tower with an armed prison guard standing at the top. I could feel watchful eyes all around us. The prison consisted of several plain white stone buildings surrounded by high chain-link fences topped with thick barbed wire. It looked very daunting, and I feared making some kind of unknown mistake trying to enter. We followed the signs, drove to the women's section of the prison, and parked. Melodi and I joined the end of a line of people that formed outside of the prison building in the heat of the Texas summer. Kelli had informed me not to bring anything in except my driver's license for identification. The line did not consist of too many people at that time. We waited about a half hour outside the building until a security guard instructed us to come in. We removed our shoes and a female security guard performed a body search on us by patting us down before we could proceed to the front desk to wait in another line. After signing in and giving them Kelli's full name, we waited about another half hour until they called our names. Then a prison guard led us to a large open room, resembling a very old-school cafeteria, and told us to sit at the next open round table to wait for Kelli. We sat there for another twenty minutes or so waiting. All the visitors adhered to the strict rules given to us as we entered the room. We could not get up and walk around the room, they told us. Even if someone stood up for more than a few seconds, a guard reprimanded that person, reminding them to sit down. We could not even switch chairs, if we wanted to, either. Only very small children could sit in the lap of a prisoner, and they did not allow physical contact between a visitor and the prisoner other than a brief hug at the beginning and end of the visit.

As Melodi and I sat at our table and waited for Kelli, we saw a new prisoner come out of a big locked iron door at the corner of the room every fifteen or so minutes, led by a security guard. We watched each one walk over to their family at one of the tables. Each prisoner, for the most part, received excited and emotional hugs as family members cried at the sight of them. Many of the prisoners cried as well when they saw the person or group who came to visit them. Several of the groups of visitors had small children there waiting to see a prisoner. Some of them just laid their heads down on the chest of their loved one somberly for a while upon greeting them. It felt very emotional watching the reactions of these people. It also felt surreal thinking how that would be us in a few minutes when Kelli came out. Melodi became very anxious waiting for her mom to arrive. We continued to look around the room and wait, mostly in silence. The room had a row of vending machines with snacks and drinks to purchase and a small area for young children to sit and read books or color with a little bucket of mostly broken crayons. The selection of books seemed quite small and in poor shape, old, worn, and tattered. Melodi and I talked quietly, observed the people in the room, and waited for about an hour before a security guard finally brought Kelli through the heavy metal door.

As instructed by a security guard when we entered the room, we stayed at the table and waited for Kelli to come to us. I saw Kelli look down the rows of tables and her face lit up with a huge smile when she spotted Melodi and me in the back of the large seating area. The security guard ushered her to us. I felt so happy to see my beautiful daughter! The three of us hugged and cried for a minute. Melodi sat with her mama in Kelli's chair, still crying. We continued to greet each other, and Kelli told me all about her life in prison so far. I had plenty of questions for her as well. Kelli, along with all the other inmates, wore a large white, long-sleeved shirt made out of canvas, and long, thick white pants, made out of the same material as the shirt, with an elastic waistband. She wore her hair long, straight, and parted down the middle. Even though her outward appearance lacked prim or dazzle, she looked so great to me! Her face glowed with joy, and she looked nice and healthy. She did not appear too thin anymore, as she had been during her drug-using days. I felt relieved seeing her just slightly chubby. She looked so beautiful, even donned in her prison garb, and wearing no makeup. She had natural beauty, inside and out. I could tell by looking at her and talking with her, that she had become a changed woman. She seemed to glow with a humble and grateful spirit.

She had asked me to bring quarters for the vending machine, so I could purchase some goodies for her. Kelli really looked forward to these treats as the prison food did not exactly taste like gourmet meals, she told me. The prisoners had to stay at the table during our visit, so I went to the vending machines and bought her a cold Dr. Pepper, a package of cookies, and some cheese crackers. She was so excited to receive the tasty junk food snacks and soda. We talked about her daily prison life routine and she told me that the meals consisted of very basic and bland foods, and that, as a prisoner, they were only given five minutes total to eat each meal. That astonished me. "How can you eat a meal in only five minutes?" I asked her. She explained the difficulty of it. She said you stuffed everything in your mouth and barely chewed, but swallowed as quickly as you could. In my curiosity I asked, "Why do you have such a short time to eat your meals?" Kelli told me that the time allotted for eating their meals is so short in order to cut down on fighting amongst the prisoners. She explained that any time the prisoners are together in large groups, fights often break out at the drop of a hat, so the prison wardens limit their time together.

Kelli said that she often passed her time in prison by writing letters and reading books. The library in prison helped her tremendously. She even attended some church services. A ministry came in to hold services in the prison every Sunday. Kelli said they had very powerful services and that she enjoyed them, but unfortunately, she avoided them most of the time. Sadly, according to Kelli, some of the prisoners took advantage of the church services and only attended them to get away with improper behavior. She explained that some female prisoners used the time in a church service to sneak in lesbian displays of affection together, without the guards noticing. I told Kelli that made me so sorry to hear that. So shameful!

Despite Kelli not attending the church services held in prison very often, she seemed to have a new fire for the Lord in her spirit. Such a fantastic blessing for this mama to see in her daughter! I knew God worked in mysterious ways and that He had been answering my prayers. She told me that she read from her Bible every day and that she prayed to and heard from the Lord on a regular basis. Not only did I see a difference in Kelli, I felt it deep in my soul. I experienced true inner peace, despite my daughter's surroundings in prison; a peace that passed all understanding. God revealed to me that even though Kelli was locked up in a maximum-security correctional facility, she experienced more freedom in her heart and soul than many people living out in the free world did, due to their addictions and spiritual bondages. Melodi and I enjoyed our visits with

Kelli.

When friends or coworkers asked me how Kelli was doing, I did not hesitate to share the fact that my daughter was currently serving time in prison. I told them that she had been managing very well, that I believed it to be God's will for her imprisonment, and asked them to pray for her. In doing so, many people opened up to me about a son, daughter, or loved one who had also been put in prison. My experiences with my daughter and my willingness to be honest and vulnerable allowed me to minister to people in a way that nobody else could. The Lord helped me to have a deeper understanding of how we truly can trust Him in all circumstances. Kelli and I experienced what it says in scripture that "God works all things together for good to those who love the Lord and are called according to His purpose" (Romans 8:28, paraphrased). He is so good to us when we put our whole life into His hands. As the Bible says in Hebrews 11:6 (NKJV), "But without faith it is impossible to please Him, for he who comes to God must believe that He is, and that He is a rewarder of those who diligently seek Him."

The Lord blessed me with another confirmation and reminder of His love and His continued work in the lives of my children when He gave me another prophetic word through one of His servants. On a Sunday afternoon, in April of 2016, one of the leaders in our church, Aaron Martinez, sent me a message on my phone. First, he explained that he did not deliver this message to me in person at church that morning due to my being on the stage singing with the praise team for most of the service.

I believe Aaron's timely words came directly from the

Lord. Mr. Martinez said, "Hi Julia! During worship this morning I felt the Lord ask me to pray for you and encourage you. I do not think that I have ever seen you without a smile on your face, but that does not necessarily mean that everything is perfect. You are a wonderful and prayerful mother, but the enemy is lying to you and feeding you untruths about that. He is attacking the very thing that makes you the most proud. Continue to resist the enemy. He knows that if he can silence the prayers of a mother through discouragement, then he has a free pass to her children. Your children are children of God. They are all special and talented with God-given abilities. Please continue to believe the promises of God. The promises that say all of your children will serve the Lord. The promises that say your children will be safe and clean. Promises that say your children will use their struggles to encourage others. As you are interceding for your children, please pray to edify and encourage yourself. Do not allow the lies of the enemy to penetrate. Take heed that His promises are true, and you are a child of God. I am praying for you and your family!"

These comforting words were a special gift that inspired and encouraged me to continue to fight the battle of the Lord for my daughter through faith and prayer. The enemy tried to creep in from time to time, like slow waters in a flood, and tell me that I failed as a mother. He did this, once again, by trying to convince me that the words of condemnation I heard in my head were not lies from him, the devil, but were my own thoughts about myself. Therefore, I received Mr. Aaron's message with extreme thanksgiving. He helped me to embrace my proper identity as a faithful child of God with no guilt or condemnation. It reminded me that God fought my battles for me. His message reminded me of the power of the Lord, as it says in the second half of the verse in Isaiah 59:19 (KJV), "When the enemy shall come in like a flood, the Spirit of the Lord shall lift up a standard against him." I thanked my friend Aaron Martinez and told him that his words were exactly what I needed to hear, and that I believed they came directly from our Lord. We all need a faithful and just Lord in our lives, and we need each other as well.

Kelli served all of her prison sentence and came home in October 2016, a year after becoming incarcerated. She experienced some horrible things while in prison, but she became an even stronger, tougher woman through her suffering. Do you think it was coincidence that Kelli was supposed to be a student in the Strong Tower ministry for a year, but rebelled and left early, and then directly went to prison and served a yearlong sentence? I do not. God knows what we need, and I am thankful that He helped me to trust His plan. Kelli's relationship with the Lord grew deeper than ever before, and a week after her release from prison, she kept her word and re-entered the drug treatment facility at Strong Tower ministry. I experienced such joyful relief and praised the Lord to see her back where she belonged.

11

Rehabilitation, a Hurricane, and a Tragedy

KELLI went back to Strong Tower Rehabilitation Center and Ministry after getting released from prison, just as she promised. I love Strong Tower! The care and training she received in Strong Tower saved Kelli's life. I am so thankful for this ministry. The pastors and the staff truly care about the men and women whom they help. The Lord works miracles through this program. Kelli stayed there for a year and four months and received the help she needed to live a blessed, disciplined, clean and sober productive life. Strong Tower helped Kelli work on issues with her physical addictions as well as her mental and emotional struggles. The staff and ministry teams helped her become disciplined, by requiring that she stick to a schedule each day that included Bible study classes, therapy groups and individual therapy, and physical labor of doing chores and cleaning different areas of the facility inside and out. They also provided church services several times a week for the community that the students in the ministry attended as well. Kelli, a gifted singer and worshipper, became part of their amazing praise team as a vocalist. Of course, she inherited the singing and worshipping gift from her mother, if I do say so myself. Kelli learned many important life lessons from Strong Tower. She learned how to maintain a healthy lifestyle by developing qualities such as self-discipline, a strong work ethic, a willingness to serve others, and determination.

While Kelli trained and stayed at Strong Tower rehab, I happily continued to raise and care for Melodi. She grew stronger and more well-adjusted each year. We talked a lot about the issues her mom went through and how they made Melodi feel. I spoke honestly with Melodi and shared my feelings of pain and disappointment in Kelli from earlier in her life, as well. Melodi missed her mom very much, but she and I grew closer each year. Our relationship felt as close as mother and daughter to me. She shared her feelings so openly and truthfully. We talked about our thoughts and emotions often and even cried together occasionally. I told Melodi that I had grown so proud of her for how well she handled the difficult times she went through with her mother. She seemed wise beyond her years. We talked about the tremendous struggles she experienced, but also how blessed her life remained, despite these unfortunate events. I knew, deep down, that she would achieve success in life, emotionally and spiritually, due to the fact that she knew how to express her emotions so completely, with total honesty and vulnerability. While Kelli continued to receive rehabilitation in Strong Tower, Melodi entered the fifth grade. She attended the elementary school where I taught in Santa Fe, Texas, about ten miles south of where she lived for most of her life with me, Papa Aaron, and her Uncle Randy.

Melodi's fifth grade school year turned out to be a rough and challenging year for our area in Galveston County, and especially for the Santa Fe community. In August of 2017, the year Melodi started her last year of elementary school, Hurricane Harvey hit the Houston and Galveston area, including League City and Santa Fe, and caused a great deal of flooding and devastation to our communities. Then, close to the end of Melodi's fifth grade school year, in May of 2018, the horrific and tragic event that became known as the "Santa Fe School Shooting" happened at the only high school in the Santa Fe school district, right around the corner from the elementary school where I taught and Melodi attended. This tragic event killed eight students and two teachers. Melodi and I experienced both the hurricane and the school shooting in a very powerful way. These events affected us deeply.

One week after school started in 2017, the Santa Fe school district sent out a message that schools needed to close early that day and would be canceled the next day, due to a hurricane predicted to make landfall later that night. Santa Fe and League City fell in the line of path that they predicted Hurricane Harvey to hit, once it made landfall. The city of Santa Fe, where I work, lies only eight miles off the Galveston Gulf Coast, and our home in League City sits about fifteen miles off of the coast. Hurricane Harvey did not form as an extremely powerful hurricane, but it had become very large and slow moving by that time. Living in the Gulf Coast region of Texas for over thirty-five years, I experienced many storms and hurricanes. Hurricane Harvey became a strange and unique storm like no other. I still shudder when I think about what this hurricane did to all Texans in the Gulf Coast area. The hurricane proceeded to hit land a little west of us the next day, late in the morning, and then bounced back down into the Gulf of Mexico. Then it unexpectantly took a turn to the east, towards Galveston, came back on land and stalled for a couple of days, just sitting over us, dumping rain incessantly. It did not cause a lot of damage with high winds like many powerful hurricanes do, but it knocked out the power for most of our area. The uniqueness of Hurricane Harvey was that it stayed in one area for about four or five days, dumping an unprecedented fifty-seven inches of rain in our region during that time. It hovered in our surrounding area and we received "the dirty side" of the hurricane, meaning it continuously poured rain on us in the outlying areas of its path, non-stop, for days on end. Schools remained canceled, businesses had closed, and we stayed in our house. Thankfully, after about a day with no power, the lights came back on in our neighborhood. We felt very lucky, as most of our city and the cities around us did not get their power back for two to three weeks. We watched helplessly as the rain continued to pour down endlessly, and we became fearful as the waters rose higher and higher up toward our house in our front and back yard toward the entryways. We could not believe it, but after days and days of rain, it finally stopped, thankfully, just short of an inch away from coming into our house. However, many homes and businesses in our area and the surrounding cities, unfortunately, did flood very badly.

Hurricane Harvey caused massive destruction to a large number of houses and buildings all around us due to high water and flooding. Many of my friends and some of my family members' houses flooded, some receiving up to five feet of water inside their homes.

My family and I sat in our house watching the local and national news stations reporting on and showing live footage of areas right around the corner from us. We saw these houses, schools, and other buildings that once stood on dry ground, but now looked like lakes. Rescue teams worked night and day all around our area helping people literally escape from drowning in their own homes. My sister's husband, my brother-in-law Ronnie, stayed in his house about ten miles from where we lived, alone, while the flooding rains inched up to a massive five feet of water inside his house. My brother-in-law had to climb up on his kitchen counter to keep from literally going under water. The poor man slept on his kitchen counter all night, thinking he would perish before daylight came. Thankfully, a rescue team drove a boat through his neighborhood calling out to people who had not evacuated, rescued him and some of his neighbors, and took them to a shelter. Another one of my sisters, Polly, and her husband Billy also watched as two or three feet of flood waters rose in their home, a few miles from where we live. The two of them tried to lift their furniture, valuables, and other sentimental items to place them upon high shelves in their home to protect them. Sadly, almost all of their possessions became destroyed in the flood, as did everything in the house of my brother-in-law Ronnie. We often think we will have time to do things like that in a disaster, but usually, that is not the case.

Other inconveniences that may not usually come to mind when thinking about effects of a flood or natural disaster happened too. For example, my mother and father's toilet did not work while enduring days of raining and flooding around their home. They live about half of a mile away from us in League City. My parents' home did not flood, but their toilets backed up, so my mom had to come over to our house after the waters receded enough to drive on the streets, so she could use our facilities. She stayed and visited with us for several hours that day. It felt so great to see my mom and know that both she and my dad made it through the hurricane okay. We made some coffee, and my mom even played a board game with me, my husband, Randy, and Melodi. We talked about the incredible situation and how sad we felt for those that the hurricane had affected much worse than us. At that time, however, it had not completely stopped raining, so we prayed for the hurricane to move on through and that our homes would not flood as well.

After stalling over our area for four days, Hurricane Harvey finally moved on out, headed north and eventually fizzled out. About two or three days later, the flood waters completely receded. Then our city, Galveston County, and the surrounding counties had a chance to assess the massive amounts of damage and destruction that mighty force of nature caused. As we watched our local and national news, we saw the reports of the devastation resulting from flooding all around us. When the flood waters lowered, I ventured out and drove around the city to look at the damage caused by Hurricane Harvey. My heart sank at what I saw. All around us in our area, you could observe a house or building and tell how high the water rose in that structure by looking at a ring around the house. The ring consisted of pieces of grass and dirt that had been floating at the top of the waters and then clung to the side of the house or building after the flood waters slowly receded when the rains finally stopped. As I drove around, I saw people coming out of their homes carrying everything, large and small, and piling it up by the streets. In some neighborhoods, every house had piles and piles, up to five and six feet high, of their personal belongings, furniture, trash, clothes, boxes of items, and more by the road. Everything became ruined in the flooding, leaving almost nothing salvageable. I drove by slowly and watched the sad process of people dragging things out, carrying things by the armload, or pushing overflowing wheelbarrows slowly through their yards and driveways. It seemed so surreal. It looked like the scene of a movie or a disaster event from the news. It did not feel like real life. As I drove by, the sorrow on the faces of the people of my city brought tears to my eyes. I knew I had to help, if I could.

The school districts canceled school, of course, but my husband's company stayed open and he continued working, thankfully. I recruited my son Randy to come help me with the clean-up at my brother-in-law's house in a neighboring city close by. We arrived late in the morning at his house and joined about six other people there helping also. These people came from my sister's church to help with the clean-up. We did not even know these folks, but in tough times, the good comes out in people. My son and I introduced ourselves to the group of workers and asked what we could do to help. I greeted my brother-in-law Ronnie, the one who stayed in the house and climbed on the counter to keep from drowning, and we hugged and cried for a couple of minutes. Before we got to work on the clean-up, he briefly told me what he went through and how he felt during the brunt of Hurricane Harvey. He described the scary scene he lived through. He recalled how he felt trapped in that house alone, with no power, while the flood waters rose all around him. He had a cell phone, he told me, and called for help, but his neighborhood streets flooded with water very early into the storm, and nobody could drive into the neighborhood to rescue him. The flood waters rose five feet up into his home during the hurricane. After losing almost all hope of survival and rescue, he climbed onto a countertop in his kitchen and laid down, not knowing what else to do. My poor brother-in-law Ronnie! It was so devastating and frightening for him. Finally, Ronnie continued, rescuers came in a boat down his street, calling out on a megaphone for people who had not evacuated. Those heroes told him that they had already made several trips by his house, but that he must not have heard their calls before he finally hearkened to them and came out. Thank God for those heroes making such extreme efforts, going around neighborhoods on a boat!

Hurricane Harvey's floods destroyed so many homes and businesses in our area. This became so incredibly costly for individuals in our cities and devastated so many. It took years, in some cases, to complete the clean-up and rebuild homes and businesses in the community. Many families and residents became temporarily displaced as they rebuilt their homes and some people even had to relocate permanently. Some of the businesses never reopened. Bubba's Seafood, a restaurant in our town of League City, Texas, where my son Randy worked, completely flooded out and did not rebuild or reopen. It took several months for my sister Pauline to restore the inside of the home she shared with her husband Billy, and it was over a year before my brother-in-law Ronnie had his home restored and he could move back in. After Hurricane Harvey hit, friends, neighbors, and even strangers turned into heroes for those in need, finding strength and comfort in each other. The outpouring of love and the help from neighbors and volunteers restored hope in humankind and pulled our communities together like never before.

Melodi and I had to miss several weeks of school due to the impact of Hurricane Harvey in Santa Fe, Texas, where I taught, and she attended. She enjoyed her three teachers and had many friends at her school. I loved having my granddaughter attend school where I worked. It gave me so much comfort to have her in a classroom only a few hallways over from where I taught my fourth graders. She walked to my classroom at the end of her school day and told me all about the events and lessons of each day. She always had a story to divulge regarding her and her friends, and it made me so content to see the joy in her eyes as she laughed about one of the funny anecdotes she had to tell. I did not realize at the time that this would be the last year that we raised Melodi full time. I sure did relish each day I spent with her! Our drive to school every day took about forty-five minutes round trip, and we enjoyed long conversations on our commutes. We talked about everything from serious moral issues, such as life lessons or Biblical stories, to silly things, like a student or classmate making a joke or having an embarrassing episode. She had also adapted some of my random humor, as I like to call it, where we find unlikely, everyday situations hilarious, when presented in a comical way. We laughed together often. Melodi and I had a special relationship that blossomed a great deal and had come a long way from where we started. She no longer blamed me or felt resentment toward me for not being able to be with her mother, as she once did. As she grew up, she came to see the harsh reality of what drugs had done to her mom, and understood that her Papa Aaron and I did Kelli a favor by raising her daughter and treating her as our own child. Our relational bond felt as close as mother and daughter, rather than grandmother and granddaughter.

Melodi's fifth grade school year in 2017/2018 started out with a challenging natural disaster, Hurricane Harvey, and unfortunately, ended with a horrific man-made tragedy for the city of Santa Fe and its community. The morning of May 18, 2018, Melodi and I headed to our school in my car at about 7:45 am. As we drove down the road toward Santa Fe, we engaged in a typical conversation about the present school day's expectations, but then became interrupted by a police car coming up from behind us, with its sirens blaring, at a very high speed. We pulled over to the side of the road and let the police vehicle go by. Then, as I continued driving, another police car came from the same direction and drove around us with loud sirens. Then another, and then another. By the time the sixth or seventh police car came speeding around us, heading toward Highway 6 in Santa Fe, I knew something very serious had occurred. Melodi and I speculated about what it could possibly be. We never even imagined the magnitude of the tragedy that took place that day, but we knew it must be something pretty bad, due to the amount of police cars zipping around us at such high speeds.

Melodi and I arrived at our school a few minutes later. I saw many more cars there than normal in the car rider drop-off line, and some kids and adults running. Melodi and I got out of our car and went into the school building. As I walked into the hallway toward my classroom, I could see a fearful and confused look in the eyes of my coworkers and some of the students. I put my things down in my classroom as Melodi headed off to the gymnasium to meet with some of her friends, before heading to her class. We hugged and said good-bye, and I watched her walk away down the hallway and turn the corner. Immediately after that, one of my students ran up to me and said, "Mrs. Savell, my mom just dropped me off, but I'm not staying. A shooting happened at the high school this morning and my mom told me to come back to her car because she doesn't want me at school right now." Then he sprinted off down the hall back toward the door where the car riders came in.

When my student told me there had been a shooting at our small school district's only high school, I thought, *This cannot be true. I am sure my student just heard a rumor. He and his mom are probably just overreacting to a false alarm. I am sure nothing really happened, or if it did, it is not as bad as they think.* This tends to be the way I always think. When I hear about bad news or the possibility of a dangerous occurrence, I switch to "the glass is half full" mode. *There must be some mistake in what they heard*, I tell myself, or *They must be exaggerating the truth. Once we find out all the facts, I believe everything will turn out okay.* From what I see, most of the time, these situations usually turn out to be better than first reported. It seems some people want to automatically think of the worst-case scenario and report it as the truth before they have all the facts or the complete story. I do not want to get extremely upset or go into panic mode for no reason, as it turns out in most cases.

Classes had not started yet, so I went across the hall into my teaching partner's classroom to talk to her and see if she had heard any news about the situation. I did not find her in her room, but I spoke to another coworker who told me what she knew at the time. My partner teacher had to leave the school and go to the high school because her daughter, who attended Santa Fe High School, texted her to report that all of the students had been evacuated from the school due to a possible active shooter in the building. After hearing this news, I still did not want to believe in a dire situation. I kept thinking to myself that, most likely, a student or person outside of the high school got caught with a gun so they evacuated all of the students and staff out of the building, just to be on the safe side. My coworkers and I talked and had many concerns about the situation. A few minutes later, the time came to go pick up our fourth-grade students from the drop-off area so we could start class. When I picked up my class, I felt surprised and concerned to only find a little more than half of my students present. I led my students down the hallway to our classroom and I could hear them whispering speculations and rumors amongst each other about a shooting incident. I knew that the children felt scared and worried, so when we arrived to our classroom and got situated, I reassured them that everything would be okay, and not to get upset about rumors they heard. A couple of the students began crying out of fear, due to having older siblings at the high school and not knowing the full story yet. I did not blame them for worrying about their older brothers and sisters, but I knew I had to help them stay calm and keep them hopeful that nothing terrible had happened. I attempted to reassure them and reminded them to try not to worry or think about it since we did not know all the facts.

About an hour later, my principal texted all of the staff and myself to inform us that there had indeed been a shooting at the high school. She told us she did not have all the details, but that there had been a fatality. I felt so upset. I could not believe this had actually happened. I still tried to hope for the best. I told myself that maybe there had just been an accidental shooting. I hoped and prayed for the best-case scenario and nothing more than that. My poor students could not concentrate on a math lesson or any other kind of lesson that day, and many of them snuck a peek at their cell phones and saw that something bad had actually happened. They felt scared, confused, and shaken, as did I. I assigned my students three options for the day, complete a lesson on their laptop computers (which I purposely made very easy), read their library book, or catch up on unfinished work. I found it pointless to try to teach the planned lesson for that day due to the small class size and the state of mind of the remaining students. As the day continued, one by one, students started getting picked up early by their parents. As the student's attendance kept dwindling down, I got a few more text messages announcing the possibility that more than one fatality had occurred at the high school, and that the authorities had begun investigating the situation. The other teachers and I met in the hallway outside of our classroom doors and discussed the horrible news in shock. After a few hours of class, most of the students in my class got picked up early and only four or five students out of twenty-one remained in my classroom. I held back my tears all day, for the sake of my students, but found it very difficult to keep from crying when I overheard one of my students say to the other kids left in the room, "If we have not gotten picked up by our parents by now, it means they do not love us." My poor babies were so scared and confused. What a horrible and tragic day!

We finally made it through the school day. I went home and immediately tuned in to the local news station on television. All the news stations reported on and showed coverage about the Santa Fe High School shooting that occurred that day. They continued the story and reports for the next several days, and it became national news as well. A seventeen-year-old male student at Santa Fe High School allegedly came to school on May 18, 2018, and killed 10 people at the high school, eight students and two teachers. This awful, senseless act of brutality became the third highest number of fatalities at a school shooting in the United States, behind the Columbine High School massacre in 1999 and the Stoneman Douglas High School shooting in 2018. The Santa Fe school district, with a total of only four schools at the time, closed all of the campuses for the next two weeks, including my school, while the community processed what had happened, and criminal investigations began. The high school students did not go back at all that school year in order to have time to grieve and receive mental counseling. Melodi and I felt utter shock. We could not believe what had happened. We still think about it and discuss that morning of May 18th, when we drove to our school at 7:45 am and the police cars sped past us to the scene of the crime taking place right down the road from where we were.

After several days, we learned the names of the victims of that horrific school shooting. Upon seeing the names of the victims, I realized that two of the names seemed very familiar to me. I did not always remember every name of my prior class rosters, as I had taught for thirteen years at that time, and usually had about forty students each year. I asked my former teaching partner if she remembered us teaching those two students in the years that we taught together. Santa Fe was a very small school district, and I knew that most of the slain victims had to come through our elementary school during their elementary years. My former teaching partner told me that one of the victims, Shana Fisher, had been in our classes as our former student. What a tragedy! She said we did not teach the other student together whose name sounded familiar to me, Christopher Stone. The elementary school opened back up to finish out the school year, a week before summer break. I could not get the name Christopher Stone out of my mind. When I went back to my classroom, I made a beeline to my file cabinet to look for my folder of class pictures I kept from all the prior years I taught. Coincidentally, the very first picture I pulled out of the file, and the very first face of the very first person I looked at in the class picture showed a young, fourth-grade Christopher Stone. I had taught him in his fourth-grade year, eight years prior to 2018, when I taught by myself as a self-contained teacher at Santa Fe Elementary South. I just sat in my classroom and cried for several minutes. The memories of Christopher all started coming back to me. I remembered Christopher as a very well-behaved child who had a heart of gold. I clearly recalled the huge smile that Chris always had on his face, and how he always made himself available to help out anyone who needed a hand, including his teacher. A few days later, I attended Chris Stone's funeral along with hundreds of other mourners. My church's associate pastor, Clint DeGroot, officiated the funeral, as he and his wife grew up in Santa Fe and knew many of the community members, as well as some of Chris Stone's family.

After "the tragedy", as we in the Santa Fe community called the incident of May 18, 2018, the people in the small rural city pulled together with prayer services and fund raisers for the family of the victims. Pastor deGroot also ministered at several of these functions and prayer vigils. The community started being known as "Santa Fe Strong". Melodi and I respectfully wear our green "Santa Fe Strong" shirts every year on May 18th in remembrance of that tragic day and in support of the families of Shana Fisher, Christopher Stone, and the rest of the victims from that horrific day of murder. The young man allegedly respons-ible was actually a student at Santa Fe High School and has been charged with capital murder of multiple persons and aggravated assault against a public servant. He is currently being held in custody without bail. If convicted, he faces a maximum sentence of 40 years to life. At the date of this writing however, the young man who allegedly committed this crime has not yet had a court trial on account of psychological tests claiming he cannot stand trial due to his mental state. This makes it very difficult for the families of the murdered victims to receive closure. I pray that they receive comfort and healing from our Lord.

12

Graduation, Restoration, and Reunification

STRONG Tower rehabilitation ministry held a graduation ceremony for Kelli after she received rehabilitation and training for one year in the center. I became one happy mama and felt extremely proud of her for staying in the program for a year and achieving the best accomplishment of her life! I invited our family and all the beautiful people in Kelli's life who loved her, supported her, and helped her achieve this outstanding goal. The ceremony took place in the sanctuary of Strong Tower Church, located in a wooded, remote area of Hitchcock, Texas. Many of the people we invited attended the joyful graduation event. This blessed occasion, by far, stands out as one of the best nights of my life, and Kelli's, too. Officer Gabe Gonzalez and Pastor Clint deGroot joined us, the two gentlemen that helped rescue and deliver Kelli from the evil spirit that plagued her. Those two heroes had also been part of the group that came to her apartment with me and helped Kelli as she packed up and got ready to go to Strong Tower the first time. Our Senior Pastors, Greg and Deena Thurstonson, came to the beautiful ceremony as well. Pastor Greg and Deena prayed for us, supported us emotionally, and counseled Kelli many times before she entered Strong Tower.

Many friends joined us that night also, including Tom and Robin Holmes, John and Michelle McHazlett, with their daughter and Melodi's best friend, Elizabeth, and one of Kelli's long-time friends, Michelle Mallios. Kendra blessed us by coming too. She is the mother of the two children Kelli adopted out. She brought the children, Reed, Reese, and Raylan to the ceremony. My wonderful mom and dad came, Kelli's grandma and grandpa, Gordon and Frances Williamson. My sisters and their husbands came, Pauline and Billy Foxx, Margie and David Dewey, and Rhonda and Ronald McCloud. Many of Kelli's cousins and her brother Randy came to the joyful occasion, as well. It just added to my joy and filled me with awe and astonishment that so many people came to her one-year graduation at Strong Tower Church that night. I give glory to God for the abundance of people who loved and supported Kelli. I loved seeing the beautiful gesture made by these folks who traveled out to the remote area to join us for this amazing ceremony. My heart overflowed with love and pride!

The Strong Tower family, the fellow students, staff, and ministry leaders also surrounded Kelli that night to honor her at the celebratory ceremony. Michael and Kendra Adams, the pastors and founders of Strong Tower Church and rehabilitation ministry, have created a treasured blessing to so many who have entered the program.

I could feel the joy of the Lord that night as we entered the beautiful sanctuary. The room felt so warm and welcoming as I looked around at the extremely high ceilings and dimmed lighting. The men in the Strong Tower rehab program sat on the left side of the sanctuary toward the front, while the women sat on the right side in the front rows. The families and guests of the honorees of that night sat on either side, behind the Strong Tower students. The ceremony began with praise and worship songs performed by Strong Tower's praise team and band. They did a beautiful job of bringing in a sweet holy atmosphere, ushering in the presence of the Lord. The congregation joined in singing as well. After the song service, the ceremony began, and Kelli and the other graduates went up on stage and sat in chairs facing the audience, next to the podium.

We enjoyed Kelli's glorious graduation ceremony. They played a short, pre-recorded video of Kelli giving part of her testimony. The staff and the pastor talked about Kelli from the podium and shared many of her accomplishments and how she had grown while in the program. Then they had a time of audience participation where Kelli's family and friends could address the graduating honorees and share personal anecdotes about Kelli. I felt amazed and overjoyed as many of our family and guests spoke on Kelli's behalf. Both of my pastors from Dominion Church stood and spoke briefly. They talked about how proud they were of Kelli and thanked the pastor of Strong Tower, Pastor Michael. All of my sisters shared on behalf of Kelli, my brother-in-law Billy, our friend Michelle, and Kelli's cousin Rhianna also spoke. My beautiful mother shared a testimony about Kelli as well. My mother, Frances Williamson, always loved and favored her granddaughter Kelli. Kelli and my mother had a very close, special bond. I became pregnant with Kelli at age eighteen when I still lived at home with my parents. Kelli's father and I did not marry and broke up shortly after I became pregnant. My mother stayed with me during Kelli's birth in the hospital, and helped me raise her for the first three years of her life. I delivered Kelli through a cesarean section birth. My mother began her testimony and praise for Kelli at the Strong Tower ceremony by saying, "I was at the birth of this beautiful granddaughter of mine, and when she came out of her mama's tummy, she came out butt-first! She really knew how to make an entrance!" The audience roared with laughter at that unexpected statement. I loved and cherished all the special stories and candid speeches given for Kelli that night! God began to give Kelli and me a double portion of blessing after all the years of struggle we had lived through. The testimonies and speeches by our loved ones were very touching, emotional, and healing. Many tears were shed, but we delighted in a great deal of laughter as well. I felt overwhelmed with pride as I watched with amazement and listened to story after story of each one's testimony of love, admiration, devotion, and honor for Kelli. When my turn came to speak during the cere- mony, I gave all the glory to our Father God for bringing her out of darkness and death, and putting her in this shining, glorious position of healing and love. I also thanked all of the wonderful people in my life who had helped bring Kelli and me through those dark years, as well as the very special pastors, staff, and friends to Kelli in

Strong Tower.

After Kelli's one-year graduation from Strong Tower, she decided to continue in the program as a junior staff member. I could not believe it. This made me so proud and brought me so much joy. Kelli's new position as junior staff gave her more responsibilities around the campus and some leadership roles over her peers in Strong Tower. It also allowed her to move out of the dormitory room that she shared with fellow students and have a room of her own there on the church's campus. Kelli felt most excited about another privilege she received from becoming a junior staff member. Melodi could now move in and share a room with Kelli on the Strong Tower campus. This huge step of having Melodi move in with her meant the world to Kelli! She had not had her now twelve-year-old daughter with her full time in years. I had been completely raising Melodi since she was fourteen months old.

Melodi moved in with Kelli and they stayed at Strong Tower for another four months, and then Kelli decided to come home and start a new chapter of her life. Aaron and I let Kelli and Melodi live with us until Kelli could get on her feet. We told her she could stay as long as she needed. Aaron and I and the whole family felt ecstatic to have Kelli back with us after her miraculous rehabilitation. I felt my joy go through the roof due to her growth and transformation. Every day I had to pinch myself to make sure that Kelli's healing had really happened. So many had collectively helped us get through that long and scary trial – the Lord, my wonderful husband, my precious family, and my sweet and loyal church friends. I thanked the Lord every day for bringing us through those years and for giving us joy and strength to fight that battle. Somehow, I even kept my sanity, amazingly!

Kelli did not waste any time getting her life going once she got home. She got a job at a restaurant right away and purchased a car after a few months. She decided she wanted to pursue training in the medical field. After researching a few avenues, she chose to get a certificate in phlebotomy. This would allow her to work in a doctor's office or in a clinic and draw blood from patients who needed blood work done. She took her courses, studied diligently, took her test, and received her certificate in about eight months. Kelli worked hard and did not stop until she achieved her goal. I knew she had changed.

Kelli and Melodi attended church with us every week at Dominion. Our friends and pastors felt just as proud of Kelli as we did. Kelli stayed strong in the Lord. She loved the praise and worship as well as the Word of the Lord from the sermons. During our worship services, Kelli often joined others in the altar section at the front of the church to freely worship God by lifting her hands and singing with joy. Kelli continues to do this to this day. Frequently, fellow parishioners comment to me about Kelli's beauty, inside and out, and the freedom of the Holy Spirit made obvious through every part of her life. Her face shines with the glory of the Lord, many people tell me, and I agree. It reminds me of the way the face of Moses shone, as described in the book of Exodus, when he came down from Mount Sanai after witnessing the literal presence of God. She stays in the atmosphere of God. She is like a new creation. Her transformation testifies of God's miraculous power!

Before long, Kelli started dating a young man. Aaron and I felt hesitant about her dating so soon. It bothered us even more to find out that she and the young man had been in a relationship in the past. She and Ben had been together for a couple of years, back when Kelli still used drugs, and they habitually used drugs together. Kelli had become pregnant with Ben's baby back then, and they had put the baby boy up for adoption several years prior. Their son is Raylan James, who lives happily with his adoptive parents, Duane and Kendra, along with Kelli's other child they adopted, Reese Harmoni.

Aaron and I worried that dating Ben could cause Kelli the temptation to go back to her old drug-using ways. We did not have any ill feelings toward Ben, we just believed it was not a good idea for Kelli, a recovered addict, to spend time with a former "drug buddy". We feared it could cause old habits to come back to the surface. Kelli worked very hard at Strong Tower to develop a new healthy lifestyle that included studying God's Word, keeping a positive mental state of being, and staying self-disciplined through manual labor. I truly believe God healed her one hundred percent, and as a result of her healing and deliverance, she does not have to label herself a "drug addict" anymore. However, God never forces a person to do anything, and if she chose to walk into the lifestyle of using drugs again, slipping back into addiction could happen. He does not constrain anyone to stay away from temptations. Thankfully, the Lord does give us blessing, guidance, protection, and wisdom when we ask for it, but a person has complete free will to walk back into an unhealthy life, if they choose. I decided to have a talk with Kelli and give her my opinion about dating a person from her past, from a time period when she used drugs. For my entire adult life, since having children, I always hoped and prayed for my son and daughters to each marry a Christian, who, first and foremost, walked in the truth of the Holy Bible and lived a godly Christian life. I prayed for their future spouses to be well-educated with a good career, and always treat them with love and respect. Of course, I also wanted each of them to marry a person with good character, wholesome values, and have love and generosity towards all mankind. I continuously prayed for the very best for my three children. I knew the Lord could provide each of them with Godly spouses, too.

I started my talk with Kelli by reminding her that Aaron and I felt so extremely proud of her progress and took delight in the measure of which she had grown. I told her we knew it took hard work and discipline to come this far in her life after what she went through with her addictions. Then I began to share my concerns about her dating Ben. I told her that as a young, amazing woman of God, she had her whole life in front of her, and I hoped she would not settle for the first man that came along. I reminded her that she could wait on the Lord to bring the right man to her. I told her we believed she could have any man she wanted and that he should be a Godly man, mature in his relationship with the Lord and have a solid foundation in life, with a good career. I shared that I wanted the very best for her and prayed for her happiness and success. I continued by telling her we felt nothing against Ben, but we did not know him that well, other than what we knew of him from the past, and had no ill feelings toward him personally. I finished by telling Kelli that her stepfather and

I just wanted her to have the very best in life, and we thought she deserved nothing but blessings and true love from a good man.

Kelli responded very respectfully. She told me she completely understood how I felt, that she knew I said these things out of love. That statement alone confirmed to me the huge growth she had made toward maturity. In the past, when I tried to give her advice, she often lashed out at me and said she did not need anyone telling her what to do. On that day, though, she continued by saying she realized that she had put our family, me in particular, through a great deal of heartache throughout her life, and that she felt truly sorry for all of the pain she had caused. Kelli told me this on several occasions since recovering from drug addiction. I knew that she really meant it and I appreciated it. I expressed to her that she should not feel any condemnation on account of her past mistakes, because I knew that she had struggled tremendously in the past, due to her addictions, and I did as well, but the Lord helped me get through those very difficult times. I told her that she could rest assured I had forgiven her and had nothing but feelings of joy, love, and hope in a bright future for her life.

Then Kelli continued, in our talk about her dating Ben, and said, "I know you are worried, Mama, and I totally understand, but I just love him so much!" After hearing her say she loved him, I knew it was too late to change the situation. I did not realize that Kelli already felt so strongly about Ben. Kelli continued by assuring me that Ben had changed. She said he did not use drugs anymore and that he had a good job. She also said that he gave his heart to the Lord and became a Christian. We hugged and I told her that

I felt very happy for her and so excited to hear the wonderful news about Ben's life now.

I talked to Aaron and told him about Kelli and Ben. We agreed that at this point we probably could not do anything to change Kelli's mind about dating Ben. We decided to keep putting all of our trust in the Lord and surrendered the situation to Him. We prayed for God's will for Kelli's life and her future. I did not have a fear about it anymore, but instead received a heavenly peace. It also helped me feel better that Kelli and Ben spent more time with us now, unlike the years in the past where Ben rarely came into our house, but just stayed out in his car in our driveway when he came over with Kelli. They started attending church together with us on Sundays, and afterwards, we often met for lunch or sat in our living room and talked and got to know Ben. In fact, we did not just learn more about Ben, but become reacquainted with Kelli as well. In all the years of Kelli using drugs, she never stuck around very long at my house or any of our family gatherings. We did not spend much time together alone, just mother and daughter either. Our relationship had begun to dissolve way back when she was only eleven years old, the time, in particular, when she first ran away from home and stayed gone for over twenty-four hours and first used pot with her friend from school. Now, she began staying at my house longer and hanging around with our family much more, and these times began a precious renewal of our mother and daughter bond of love and friendship that we lost so long ago. Yes, Ben and Kelli's past lives did not give us much reason to believe they had a good future together, but I knew we could trust in God, because He made all things possible. I knew in my heart that the Lord made it His business to heal and restore lives and relationships. I laid my worries, doubts, and fears about Kelli at the feet of Jesus through prayer, and He exchanged my burdens for sweet peace. What an amazing God!

Five months later, in October 2019, Ben and Kelli married in Galveston, Texas, with Aaron, me, and Melodi as witnesses. They had a nice ceremony at the Galveston County Courthouse, officiated by the Justice of the Peace. Kelli found a beautiful, white, spaghetti strap dress that clung to her waist, with a silky, layered, flowing skirt which hung down just below her knees. Ben wore nice jeans and a white, short-sleeved polo shirt. They both wore white Converse Allstars tennis shoes. They looked perfectly matched and so cute together! Kelli and Melodi carried small, fall-colored bouquets that I made and tied with a wide, dark-brown ribbon. I pinned a nice rose boutonniere to Ben's shirt while we stood outside in front of the courthouse before the ceremony. The ceremony took place on a beautiful fall day in Galveston, and afterwards we took several pictures by a large, gorgeous fountain, right outside of the courthouse by the Gulf waters of Galveston.

After the wedding, Kelli and Melodi moved in with Ben in a home very close to Aaron and me in League City, Texas. The three of them continued to attend church with us every week at Dominion Church. I felt so happy and blessed that they stayed close to us! We get to see them often. I feel thankful that Melodi can continue growing up in the area where she started out with Aaron, me, and her Uncle Randy as a small toddler.

Things are not always perfect for the new family, Kelli,

Ben, and Melodi, but they continue to work on their relationships the best they can. Our large extended family gathers together often as well. Kelli is now getting close to her cousins and aunts and uncles once again. She lingers at our family functions and enjoys time with family instead of avoiding us for various other activities, like before. Unfortunately, in the summer of 2020, we lost my beautiful mother, the matriarch of our large, close-knit family, Frances Williamson. She passed away after battling cancer for over five years. Everyone in the family shared a close relationship with my mother, especially Kelli and Melodi. My mother hosted most of our family holiday parties in her home, the house where I grew up, and planned most of the birthday parties for my sisters, me, and all her beloved grandchildren. The whole family chose to live in areas close to my parents' home, in southeast Texas. My mom hung on to life for six years after her cancer diagnosis. She suffered greatly, especially in the last few months of her life, and lost a significant amount of weight. In the last few days prior to her passing, she could not get out of bed. Most of the extended family came to her bedside, visited with her, and loved on her before she slipped away.

Two days before my mother's death, my dad and I sat with her on the edge of her bed, opposite each other, with my sweet mom lying in the middle. That became the last day she had enough strength to talk with anyone. My beautiful mother requested that I read aloud to her the first chapter of this book, a manuscript at the time, presently being read by you. My mother encouraged and supported me in the writing of this book to tell the amazing testimony of Kelli's survival and healing from the trials and battles in life with mental illness and addiction. My mother lived through it with us and helped Kelli amid her life's journeys and battles. My amazing mother, Frances Williamson, never gave up on Kelli, and fought tirelessly for her recovery. I will always treasure those beautiful, emotional moments at my mother's bedside before her passing, as I read from the pages of this book to Mom and Dad, and watched as they both became moved to tears. I finished reading chapter one and then explained the premise of the rest of the book and the progress I had made up to that point. My mother encouraged me with compliments on the writing of the story so far. It made me so happy to receive my mother's blessing in writing this book before her death. I knew she felt very proud of me, and of Kelli as well.

My mother loved Kelli and all nine of her grandchildren so much, as well as her ten (at the time of this writing) great-grandchildren. She especially favored her great-granddaughter, Melodi. The two of them had a very special and close relationship. When I obtained physical custody of Melodi at just over a year old, my mother stepped in to help us a great deal through the years of her life. Melodi, the first great-grandchild of my mom and dad, stayed with them often as a little girl. My mom chose "Great Grams" and "Great Gramps" as the great-grandparent titles for her and my dad. My mother loved to tell the story of the difficulty little Melodi had as a toddler pronouncing "Great Grams" and "Great Gramps" correctly. She called both my mom and dad "Gate Gams". When my mom asked Melodi if she meant Great Grams or Great Gramps, Melodi would reply, "I mean Gate Gams, the boy one" when talking to my dad, or, "You're Gate Gams, the girl one," when referring to my mom. My mom laughed every time she shared that memory. Melodi meant the world to her.

On the morning of July 14, 2020, my father called Kelli, asking her to come to his home to check on her grandmother. Kelli confirmed what my father feared, that, indeed, she had no pulse and had left us. How precious to me to know that my sweet mother stood by my side in the delivery room while Kelli entered this world during her birth, and now, Kelli stood by her grandmother's bedside at the time my beloved mother left this earth and entered into eternity to be with our Heavenly Father. My mother and Kelli had such a beautiful relationship! She lovingly referred to Kelli as her "Pee Wee" from the time of her premature birth, due to her tiny size, and throughout her whole life.

Many of the family and I gathered at my mom and dad's house that morning, after she died peacefully in her own bedroom. We stayed with my dad to comfort him and mourn together. As an extremely close family, several of us met there each day and lingered together in the family room of my parents' house, visiting with each other and sharing memories for the next several days. Although we felt so sad and heartbroken at the death of my sweet mother, our time together helped begin the healing process. We cried a great deal, but we also laughed, reminiscing about our lives' stories and the times we had with a truly amazing woman, our mother, grandmother, great-grandmother and wife, Frances.

My niece Melissa and her husband Michael welcomed another child into their family a few weeks after my mom passed away. Melissa and Michael decided to wait until after the baby's birth before they or anyone else found out its gender. During Melissa's pregnancy, my mother asked to see the gender report of Melissa's baby, not knowing how much longer she had here on earth. She kept the secret but knew that her tenth great-grandchild was a baby girl before anyone else in the family. Sadly, she did not live to see sweet little baby June, who came into the world on July 25, 2020, eleven days after she passed.

A few months later, after celebrating their first wedding anniversary, Kelli and Ben decided to try to add to the family as well. Ironically, Kelli and Ben had already had a child together back in their past when they both functioned in unhealthy lifestyles. Their little boy had been adopted by Duanne and Kendra through the adoption agency, New Life Center, and Ben had never met his son, Raylan. Kelli spent time with Raylan a couple of times a year, along with Reese, her daughter, who had also been adopted by the same couple. The adoptive parents and Kelli knew each other well. They saw how Kelli had recovered from drug addictions and grew to love her and think of her as part of their family. They graciously offered to let Raylan and Reese stay with Kelli and Ben for a couple of nights, allowing Ben another opportunity to meet his son. Ben did so great with little Raylan. They all spent a nice time together, and Melodi loved seeing her half-brother and sister.

Kelli asked me to pray for her and Ben as they hoped to conceive a child. About two or three months after we started praying, I received the exciting news that my next new grandbaby would arrive sometime in May of 2021. Kelli and Ben pray they will have a baby boy. They know

God has blessed them in so many ways and they feel thrilled about the new doors opening for them. Every day I too feel in total awe of our amazing Lord. Kelli, Melodi, and I witnessed the incredible and great things He has done! I want to publicly say, "Thank You," to the God who saves, the God who provides, the God of healing, the God of deliverance, the God of freedom! Praise You for being our Comforter! Bless Your name for picking us up out of the miry clay and setting our feet on solid ground. I worship You because You gave us beauty for ashes and You gave us strength instead of fear. I have confidence that the name of the Lord is a strong tower and the righteous can run into it and be saved. If I had not found the Lord Jesus, I do not know where I would be. I sure do not know where Kelli would be! Thank you, everlasting Father and lifter of our heads. I see Your beauty, Lord, as the gentle rain that falls on a spring day and the sun that shines through the fall foliage. Precious Lord, I know you can do anything. Thank you for everything You have done!

As you, gentle reader of this book, come to the end of reading the testimony of the lives of me, my amazing daughter, and my sweet granddaughter, all saved by God's grace, I encourage you to give your life to the Lord and trust in Him, and He will do more than you can ever think or imagine. Do not give up on your loved ones. Our heavenly Father will carry them through the challenging times and deliver them too, if you put all your trust in Him. He will even bless you with joy unspeakable while you wait!

As the mother of my beautiful, saved, healed, miraculously delivered daughter, I have the privilege of hosting the baby's gender reveal party for Kelli and Ben in my home tomorrow. A pink symbol will represent they are having a girl, and blue will indicate it is a boy. Precious big sister Melodi and the rest of our family and friends will be our guests as well. The big reveal will come from a large, wrapped box I filled with balloons. Kelli, Ben, and Melodi will open the box at the party to reveal the baby's gender. I cannot wait to see their joy and surprise when they remove the lid and watch the blue balloons come floating out, announcing the arrival of their baby boy!

They that wait upon the Lord shall renew their strength. They shall rise up with wings as eagles. They shall run and not be weary, they shall walk and not faint.

Isaiah 40:31 (KJV)

About the Author

Julia Savell received her Bachelor of Science degree in early childhood education from the University of Houston. She is a public school teacher in Texas. She and her husband have four adult children and seven grandchildren. Her passion is music and she and her husband are members of their local church's praise and worship team. Julia's hobbies include bicycling and kayaking in the bayous and lakes of the Gulf Coast region of Texas.

Resources

Dominion Church
Assemblies of God Church
Pastors Greg and Deena Thurstonson
6400 Calder Drive, Dickinson, TX 77539
http://dominionchurch.org/
(281) 337-0037

Strong Tower Ministries
Non-Denominational Church and Twelve-Month
Residential Program
Pastors Michael and Kendra Adams
7801 Burns Street, Hitchcock, TX 77563
http://www.urmystrongtower.com/
(409) 440-8078

New Life Adoptions
11439 Spring Cypress Rd Building C, Tomball, TX 77377
https://www.newlifeadopt.com
(281) 955-1001

Made in the USA
Columbia, SC
12 July 2022